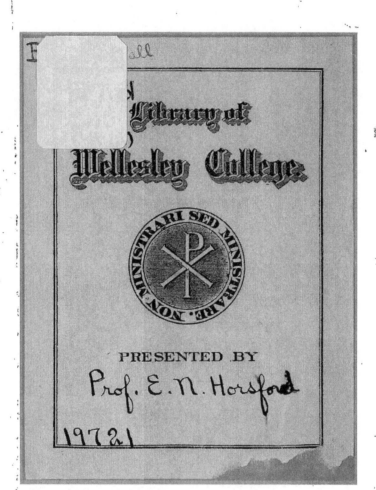

# FREDERIC CHOPIN

*HIS LIFE, LETTERS, AND WORKS.*

# FREDERIC CHOPIN

## HIS LIFE, LETTERS, AND WORKS

BY

MORITZ KARASOWSKI.

𝔚𝔦𝔱𝔥 𝔓𝔬𝔯𝔱𝔯𝔞𝔦𝔱.

*TRANSLATED FROM THE GERMAN BY*

EMILY HILL.

"Chopin is and remains the boldest and proudest poetic spirit of the age."—
ROBERT SCHUMANN

IN TWO VOLUMES.—VOL. II.

LONDON:

WILLIAM REEVES, 185, FLEET STREET,
*Publisher of Musical Works.*

1879.

G. HILL, STEAM PRINTER,

WESTMINSTER BRIDGE ROAD,

LONDON.

## CHAPTER XI.

*FURTHER SOJOURN IN VIENNA. THE JOURNEY TO MUNICH.*

Frederic Chopin to Elsner.

*Vienna, January 16th, 1831.*

Dear Monsieur Elsner,

I much regret that your kindness, of which I have had so many proofs during my journey, has once more made me feel ashamed of myself, and that you have anticipated me with a letter.

I should have felt it my duty to write to you immediately on my arrival, but I put off doing so from day to day, feeling almost certain that my parents would not delay sending you all the news about me, as I am vain enough to think this would interest you.

I wanted also to wait till I could tell you something definite about myself; but since the day on which I heard of the terrible events in the fatherland, I have had but one thought—anxiety and yearning about my country and my dear ones.

Herr Malfatti has been vainly endeavouring to persuade me that an artist is, or ought to be, a cosmopolitan. Supposing this to be so, although I was an artist in the cradle, I am, as a man, a Pole, and liable to serve as a soldier, so I hope that you will not blame me for not having thought seriously as yet about arranging for a concert.

Obstacles surround me on all sides; not only has a succession of the most miserable concerts quite ruined good music, and rendered the public distrustful, but the recent affairs in Poland have a prejudicial effect on my position.

I think, however—and Würfel fully approves my intention—of giving my first concert during the Carnival. The worthy Würfel is a constant sufferer. I often see him, and find that he has a pleasant recollection of you.

I should feel little satisfied with my stay here but for the interesting acquaintances I have made among the first talent in the place, such names as Slawick, Merk, Bocklet, &c. The opera is good, and the Viennese are enchanted with Wildt and Fräulein Heinefetter; but it is a pity that Duport brings out so few new operas, and is more careful of his pocket than of art.

Abbé Stadler * is loud in his complaints, and says

---

* Maximilian Stadler, born at Molk, in Lower Austria, August 4th, 1748, was an excellent pianist and organist. His ecclesiastical compositions were extremely popular in Vienna. In the last years of his life he was much occupied in writing on art, history, and science. He died universally esteemed and beloved in Vienna, November 8th, 1833.

that Vienna is not what it used to be.  He is publishing his Psalms at Mechetti's ; I saw the work in manuscript and admired it.

As to your quartet, Joseph Czerny promised faithfully that it should be ready on St. Joseph's day. He assured me that up till now it had been impossible for him to put it in hand, as he is just bringing out Schubert's works, many of which are still in the press.  So I am afraid that yours will be delayed.

As I observed, Czerny is not one of the wealthiest publishers in this city, and cannot so easily take the risk of printing a work that is not performed either at " Sperl's " or at the " Römische Kaiser."

Waltzes are here called " works," and Lanner and Strauss, who play first violin at the performances of these dances, " capellmeister " (band-masters.)

I do not mean to say that this is the universal way of speaking, for there are many who ridicule it ; however, scarcely anything but Waltzes are printed. It seems to me that Mechetti is of an enterprising turn of mind, and that he will be more likely to take your Masses, for he intends to publish the scores of the famous church composers.  I spoke about those glorious Masses of yours to Mechetti's book-keeper— an impressible and enlightened Saxon—he seemed to think something of them, and, according to what I hear, he does quite as he likes in the business.  I am invited out to dinner to-day to meet Mechetti. I shall talk the matter over seriously with him, and will write to you about it soon. Haslinger is now publishing Hummel's last Mass, for he lives only for and by Hummel; but it is said that these latest compositions do not sell well; and Haslinger, who gave him a large honorarium for them, puts aside all manuscripts now, and only prints Strauss's compositions.

Yesterday I was with Nidecki, at Steinkeller's, who has written a libretto for Nidecki. He hopes for great things from this opera, in which the famous comedian, Schuster, is to appear. In this case, Nidecki may make a name for himself. I hope that this news will please you.

You ask, dear Mons. Elsner, why Nidecki studied my second concerto? He did so solely by his own wish. Knowing that he would have to play in public before his departure from Vienna, and having nothing suitable of his own, except the beautiful variations, he asked for my manuscripts. Meanwhile things have greatly changed; he no longer appears as a pianoforte *virtuoso*, but as an orchestral composer. He will be sure to tell you of it himself. I shall take care that his overture is performed at my concert. You will be proud of us yet; at any rate you shall not be ashamed of us. The pianist, Aloys Schmitt, has been cut up by the critics, although he is past forty, and has been composing for eighteen years.

Kindest remembrances to all the collegians, and to your own circle. For yourself, I beg you to receive the assurance of the unbounded respect with which I always remain,

Your grateful and faithful pupil,

FREDERIC CHOPIN.

*Vienna, May 14th,* 1831.

MY BELOVED PARENTS AND SISTERS,

I have to go on short commons this week, as regards letters, but I console myself with the thought that I shall hear from you again next week, and wait patiently, trusting that you are as well in the country as you were in town. As to myself, I am in excellent spirits, and feel that good health is the best comforter in misfortune.

Perhaps it is Malfatti's soups which have given me such strength that I really feel better than ever. If so it is a two-fold regret to me that Malfatti and his family are gone into the country. You cannot imagine what a beautiful villa he lives in; I was there a week ago with Hummel. Having taken us over his house, he showed us his garden, and when we were at the top of the hill we had such a splendid view that we did not want to come down again. Malfatti has the honour of a visit from the court every year, and I should not wonder if the Duchess of Anhalt-Cöthen, who is a neighbour of his, envies him his garden.

On one side you see Vienna lying at your feet, and looking as if Schönbrunn were joined to it; on the

other, high hills picturesquely dotted with convents
and villages. This romantic panorama makes you
quite oblivious of the nearness of the noisy, bustling
Kaiserstadt.

Yesterday I was at the Imperial library with
Handler.* Do you know this is my first inspection
of what is, perhaps, the richest collection of musical
manuscripts in the world? I can scarcely imagine
that the library in Bologna can be larger and more
systematically arranged than this one.

Now, my dearest ones, picture to yourselves my
astonishment at beholding among the new manuscripts a book entitled " Chopin."

It was a pretty large volume, elegantly bound; I
thought to myself, I have never heard of any other
musician named Chopin, but there was a certain
Champin, and perhaps there has been a mistake
in the spelling. I took out the manuscript and saw
my own handwriting. Haslinger had sent the
original of my variations to the library. This is
an absurdity worth remembering.

Last Sunday there was to have been a grand display of fireworks, but the rain spoilt it. It is a
remarkable fact that it almost always rains here
when they are going to have fireworks. This
reminds me of the following story: " A gentleman
had a handsome bronze-coloured coat, but whenever

---

* An author and musical *connoisseur*, born in 1792, died
of cholera September, 1831.

he wore it, it rained; so he went to his tailor to ask him the reason. The tailor was very much astonished, shook his head, and asked the gentleman to leave the coat with him for a day or two, as, possibly, the hat, waistcoat or boots might be the cause of the misfortune. However, it was not so, for when the tailor went out for a walk in the coat the rain suddenly poured down, and the poor man was obliged to take a cab, for he had forgotten his umbrella. Some people thought his wife had taken it to a coffee-party; but, however that may have been, the coat was wringing wet. After thinking over this strange occurrence for a long time it occurred to the tailor that perhaps there was something strange hidden in the coat. He took out the sleeves, but found nothing; he undid the tails, then the front, when, lo and behold! under the lining was a piece of a hand-bill about some fireworks. This explained all; he took out the paper, and the coat never brought down any more rain." Forgive me for again having nothing new to tell you about myself; I shall hope to have some more interesting news bye and bye. I most sincerely desire to fulfil your wishes; hitherto, however, I have found it impossible to give a concert. What do you think of General Dwernicki's victory at Stoczek?

May God continue to fight for us!

Your FREDERIC.

*Vienna, May 28th,* 1831.

I have just returned from the post, but once more
there is no letter for me! I received one on Wednesday from Madame Jarocka, with a postcript from
dear Papa, which though very short was very precious to me. It told me, at least, that you were all
well. As to Marcel and Johann, I beg that they
will not write to me at all, if they are so stingy, that
in spite of my request they can only send a word or
two. I am so angry that I feel as if I could send
back their letters without opening them. Of course
they will make the old excuse of want of time! I
am the only one who has time to write so fully every
week. But how quickly this precious time passes.
It is already the end of May, and I am still in
Vienna, and probably shall be through June, for
Kumelski* has been ill and must lay by again.

I can see already that this letter will be a very
wearisome one, but you have no reason to fear that
this is a sign of indisposition. On the contrary, I
am quite well and amusing myself capitally. To-
day I was playing from early in the morning till two
in the afternoon, when I went out to dine and met
the worthy Kandler, who kindly offered to give me
letters to Cherubini and Paër.

I shall visit my invalid in the evening and go
to the theatre, where there is to be a concert at

* An esteemed friend, who was to accompany Chopin to Paris.

which the violinist Herz is to perform.  He is, an Israelite, and made his *début* at Fraulein Henriette Sonntag's concert in Warsaw, when he was almost hissed off the stage.  The pianist, Döhler, is also to play some of Czerny's compositions, and in con-clusion Herz will give his own variations on Polish airs.  Poor Polish motives, you little think how they will over-lard you with "Majufes" (Jewish melodies), giving you the title of " Polish music" to attract the public.

If you are honest enough to distinguish between real Polish music and these imitations of it, and to assign a higher position to the former, you are thought crazy, more especially as Czerny, who is the oracle of Vienna, has not, as yet, in the manufacture of his musical tit-bits, included any variations on a Polish theme.

Yesterday afternoon I went with Thalberg to the Evangelical church, where Hesse, a young organist from Breslau, was to perform before the most select of Viennese audiences.  The *élite* of the musical world were present : Stadler, Kiesewetter, Mosel, Seyfried, and Gyrowitz.  Hesse has talent, and understands the management of the organ ; he left an album with me, but I don't feel as if I had originality enough to write anything in it.

On Wednesday I was at Beper's with Slawick till 2 o'clock in the morning.  He is one of the artists here with whom I am really on friendly and con-fidential terms.  He plays like a second Paganini, whom, in time, he gives promise of surpassing. I should not think so, had I not already heard him several times. I am very sorry that Titus has not made Slawick's acquaintance, for he bewitches his hearers, and moves them to tears; he even made Tiger weep; Prince G. and Jskr. were much affected by his playing.

How are things going on with you? I am always dreaming of you. Has not the bloodshed ceased yet? I know what your answer will be: "Patience." I constantly console myself with the same thought.

On Thursday there was a *soirée* at Fuchs's, when Limmer, one of the best artists here, introduced some of his own compositions for four violoncellos. Merk, as usual, made them more beautiful than they really were by his playing, which is so full of soul. We stayed there till 12 o'clock, for Merk enjoyed playing his Variations with me. He told me so himself, and it is always a great pleasure for me to play with him. I think we suit each other very well.* He is the only violoncellist I really respect.

I am curious to know how I shall like Norblin; †
please do not forget the letter to him.

---

* Chopin dedicated to Merk his "Introduction et Polonaise Brillante pour piano et violoncello," (op. 3.)

† M. L. Peter Norblin, born in Warsaw, 1781, was first violoncellist at the Grand Opera in Paris, and teacher at the Conservatoire. He died 1852.

*Vienna, June 25th,* 1831.

I am quite well, and that is all that I have to be
happy about, for my departure seems as far off as
ever. I have never been in such a state before.
You know how undecided I am, and then obstacles
meet me at every step. I am promised a passport
every day, and I run from Herod to Pontius Pilate
simply to get back what I gave the police to take
care of. I received a delightful piece of news to-
day, that my passport had been mislaid somewhere
and could not be found, so I must try to procure a
new one. It is strange that every possible misfortune happens just now to us poor Poles. Although
I am quite ready to start, I cannot.

I have followed Herr Beyer's advice and had my
passport *viséd* for England, although I am only going
to Paris. Malfatti will give me a letter of introduction to his friend, Paër ; Kandler has already mentioned me in the " *Leipziger Musikzeitung.*"

I was not home until midnight yesterday, for
it was St. John's Day, and Malfatti's birthday.
Mechetti wished to give him a surprise, and had
engaged Mlles. Emmering and Lutzer, and Messrs.
Wildt, Cicimara, and your Frederic to give a musical
performance in his honour. This almost deserved to
be described as perfect (" parfait.") I never heard
the Quartet from " Moses " given better ; although
Fräulein Gladkowska sang " Oh quante lacrime "
with far more feeling at my farewell concert at

Warsaw. Wildt was in excellent voice, and I acted as *quasi* conductor.*

A considerable crowd was on the terrace of our house, listening to the concert. The moon shone marvellously, the fountains rose like columns of pearls, the air was filled with the perfume of the orange grove ; in short, it was an enchanting night, the surroundings glorious!

I will now describe the room in which we performed. Windows, reaching from the ceiling to the floor, open on to the terrace, from whence there is a magnificent view over the whole of Vienna. Large mirrors hung on the walls ; but the room was dimly lighted which heightened the effect of the moonlight streaming through the windows ; and the roominess of the "cabinet" adjoining the *salon* on the left gave to the whole dwelling an air of grandeur. The open-heartedness and politeness of the host, the gay and elegant company, the sparkling wit, and the excellent supper, made it late before we separated. I live as frugally as possible, and look at every penny as I did at the ring † when I was in Warsaw. You may as well sell it, for I have cost you enough already.

---

* "Cicimara said, there was no one in Vienna, who accompanied as well as I did. I thought to myself, I have been convinced of this a long time. Hush."—(Remark of Chopin's.)

† The ring presented by the Emperor Alexandra I. See Chap. III.

The day before yesterday we were on the Kahlen and Lepoldsberg with Kumelski; and Czapek, who visits me every day and gives me most substantial proofs of his friendship ; he offered to lend me money for travelling, if I wanted it. It was a magnificent day, and I never took a more beautiful walk. From the Leopoldsberg you see the whole of Vienna, Agram, Aspern, Pressburg, and even Kloster-Neuburg, the castle in which Richard Cœur de Lion was for some time imprisoned. We had a view also of all the upper part of the Danube. After breakfast we went to the Kahlenberg, where King John Sobieski pitched his camp and sent up the rockets which were to announce to Count Starhemberg, Commandant of Vienna, the approach of the Polish army. There, too, is the monastery of the Kamedules, where, before the attack of the Turks, the King knighted his son Jacob, and himself officiated in the Mass. I have gathered a leaf for Isabella from the spot which is now covered with vegetation.

From thence we went, in the evening, to the beautiful valley of Krappenwald, where we saw a ridiculous boyish frolic, a number of urchins had covered themselves, from head to foot, with leaves, and, looking like walking-bushes, crawled from inn to inn. A boy, covered with leaves, his head adorned with branches, is called " Easter-king." This is a customary jest at Easter-tide.

A few days ago I was at a *soirée* at Aloys

Fuchs's.* He showed me his rich collection of autograph works (circa 400.) My Rondo † for two pianos was among them. Some of the company present were desirous of becoming personally acquainted with me. Fuchs gave me a specimen of Beethoven's handwriting.

Your last letter gave me great pleasure, for I saw the handwriting of all my nearest and dearest ones on one piece of paper. Let me kiss your hands and feet, which are more charming than any to be found in Vienna.

*Vienna, Saturday, July* 1831.

I saw from your last letter, my dearests, that you have already learnt to bear misfortune with fortitude. You may be assured that neither am I so readily cast down. Hope, oh, sweet perennial hope!

---

* Aloys Fuchs, born 1799 in Austrio-Silesia, was for some time musical historiographer and antiquarian at the Austrian Royal Chapel. He possessed a great many autographs and portraits; and scores of the masters of the sixteenth and seventeenth centuries; also Mozart's compositions, in his own handwriting. Fuchs played the violoncello very well, and was one of Beethoven's intimate friends. At the sale of Beethoven's property, Fuchs bought, among other manuscripts, one of the sketch books, which he sent, as a mark of respect, to Mendelssohn. Another of these books was bought by Meyerbeer's brother, William Beer. Fuchs's fine collection was dispersed at his death, in 1852.

† This Rondo appeared among the posthumous works, as op. 73.

I have got my passport at last, but have given up the idea of starting on Monday. We shall go to Salzburg on Monday and from there to Münich. I asked for my passport to be *viséd* for London ; and the police did it at once ; but it was kept two days at the Russian Embassy, and was sent back with permission to travel to Münich, not to London. It is all the same to me, if Herr Maison the French Ambassador will sign it. To these troubles another has now been added. A certificate of health is necessary for crossing the Bavarian frontier, on account of the cholera. We ran about for half a day with Kumelski, but got the pass in the afternoon.

We had the pleasure of being at least in good company during our peregrinations, for Count Alexander Fredro,* whom we recognized from his Polish appearance, his refined manner of speaking, and his passport, was with us seeking a similar pass for his servant.

The news to-day is that the town of Wilna is taken. It is to be hoped this is not true.

Everyone is terribly afraid of the cholera, and the precautions taken are quite ridiculous. Printed

---

* Alexander Count Von Fredro, born 1793, celebrated as a writer of excellent comedies, and called by his countrymen, the Polish Molière, began his literary labours with a translation of Goethe's " Clavigo." His comedies sparkle with original ideas, and are an ornament to the national stage. He died at Lemberg, July 14th, 1876.

prayers are sold, supplicating God and all the saints
to stop the cholera. Nobody ventures to eat fruit,
and most people quit the city.

I leave a Polonaise for the Violoncello with
Mechetti.

Louise writes that Herr Elsner is very pleased
with the review; I am anxious to hear what he will
say about the others, as he was my teacher of composition. I want nothing but more life and spirit.
I often feel low-spirited, but sometimes as cheerful
as at home. When I feel melancholy I go to
Madame Schaschek's, where I generally meet several
amiable-young Polish ladies who always cheer me
up with their kind and hopeful words, so that I begin
to mimic the generals here. This is my last new
trick; those who have seen it are ready to die with
laughter. But there are days, alas! when people
do not get two words out of me; then I generally
spend thirty kreuzers in going to Hitzing, or somewhere else in the neighbourhood of Vienna (for
recreation) to divert my mind. Zacharkiewicz, of
Warsaw, was with me, and when his wife saw me at
Schaschek's their astonishment knew no bounds at
my looking such a proper fellow. I have only left
my whiskers on the right cheek, and they grow very
well; there is no occasion to have them on the left,
as you always sit with your right to the public.

The good Würfel was with me the day before
yesterday; Czapck, Kumelski, and several others
also came, and we went together to St. Veit, a

pretty place, which is more than I can say of Tivoli,
where there is a kind of Caroussel, or rather a rail
with sledges, called a " Rutsch." It is a childish
amusement, but a crowd of grown persons let themselves roll down the hill in these sledges without the
least object in going. At first I did not at all
care about trying; but as we were eight of us and
all good friends, we began to dare each other to
go down first. It was very foolish, but we all
laughed heartily. I went heart and soul into the
fun till it occurred to me that strong healthy men
might find some better employment at a time like
the present when there is such a universal need for
protection and defence. Confound our frivolity.

A little while ago Rossini's " Siege of Corinth "
was exceedingly well given, and I was very pleased
to have another chance of hearing the opera. Fräulein
Heinefetter, Messrs. Wildt, Binder, and Forti, in a
word, all the best artists in Vienna, were present
and did their utmost. I went to the opera with
Czapek, and when it was over we went to the same
restaurant where Beethoven used to take his supper.

I must say, in case I forget, that I shall probably
take rather more money from Peter the banker than
dear papa had arranged for. I am very economical,
but heaven knows I can only do as I am doing, or I
should set off with an empty purse. God keep me
from illness; but if anything did happen to me, you
might, perhaps, reproach me for not having taken
more. Forgive me, and remember that I have lived

o

on this money during May, June, and July, and that I have to pay more for my dinner now than in winter. I am doing this not merely of my own accord, but on the good advice of others. I am very sorry to be obliged to ask you. Papa has already spent more than a penny on me, and I know how difficult money is to earn. Believe me, my dearests, it is as hard for me to ask as it is for you to give. God will help us *punctum*.

It will be a year in October since I received my passport; it will need, of course, to be renewed; how shall I manage it? Write and say if you can send me a fresh one. Perhaps that is impossible.

I often run out and visit Hans or Titus. Yesterday I could have sworn I saw the latter in front of me, but I found it was only a confounded Prussian!

It is to be hoped these expressions will not give you a bad impression of the manners I have learnt in Vienna. There is nothing particular about the style of talk here, except that they say "Gehorsamer Diener" (your obedient servant) in taking leave, and pronounce it "Korschamer Diener." I have acquired no habit that is truly Viennese; for instance, I cannot play any waltzes, and that is proof enough.

God give you health. May no more of our friends fall. Poor Gustav!

I dine to-day with Schaschek; I shall wear the studs with the Polish eagles, and use the pocket-handkerchief with the Kosynier.

I have written a Polonaise, which I must leave here with Würfel. I received the portrait of our commander-in-chief, General Skrzynecki, but frightfully spoilt, on account of the cholera. Your letters have also been cut, and each bears a large sanitary stamp; so great is the anxiety here.

In the last letter, or rather in a few lines, dated July 20th, 1831, Frederic informs his parents that he is going to start the same day with Kumelski, for Münich, through Linz and Salzburg. He writes that he is well, and provided with money, but fears that it will not last out, and asks for some more to be sent to Münich.

These are all that remain of the large collection of Chopin's letters preserved by his parents. To the fate which befell the other letters I will refer in the following chapter.

# CHAPTER XII.

AFTER Chopin's death, his effects were sold by auction in Paris, and the furniture of his two *salons*, with the souvenirs he had delighted to have around him, were bought by Miss Stirling, a Scotch lady, one of his pupils and enthusiastic admirers. She took them home with her, and they formed a kind of Chopin Museum.   This interesting collection included a portrait of the gifted artist, painted by his friend, Ary Schäffer; a grand piano, by Pleyel, on which Chopin had generally played ; a service of Sèvres porcelain, with the inscription, " Offert par Louis Philippe à Frédéric Chopin, 1839 ; " a splendid and costly casket, presented by Rothschild ; and carpets, table-covers, and easy chairs, worked by Chopin's pupils.

Miss Stirling directed, in her will, that when she died these relics were to be sent to Chopin's mother, to whose house in Warsaw they were accordingly conveyed in 1858.   After the death of Madame Chopin, in 1861, they passed into the hands of her daughter, Isabella Barcinska. This lady occupied the second floor of one of two houses standing exactly on the boundary between the "New World," and the "Cracow Suburbs, and belonging to Count Andreas Zamoyski.

At the commencement of the political disturbances, which preceded the insurrection of January, 1863, a band of excited young men, inflamed by opinions which were far from being shared by the public, conspired to murder all the deputies. Although the miserable schemes of these fanatical patriots completely failed, they continued to contrive fresh ones, till, at length, exasperated beyond endurance by the bloody conflict which raged through the whole country, they laid a plot to take the life of Count von Berg, who, on the recall of Prince Constantine, had become supreme governor of Poland. Count Berg was returning in his carriage, on the 19th September, 1863, at six in the evening, with an escort of Circassians, from the Belvedère to the Palace. When the carriage came to the spot where the "New World" and "Cracow Suburb" adjoin, a shot, followed by some Orsini bomb-shells, was fired from a window on the fourth floor of Count Zamoysk's house. The street was immediately in an uproar, but no one was killed, and only a horse or two belonging to the escort wounded. A detachment of the military, who were at that time always kept in marching order on the Saxon Square, came up in a few minutes. The soldiers surrounded both houses, rudely dragged out the women, and left them in the road, while the men were sent, under a military convoy, to the citadel.

As lava pouring forth from a volcano uproots and annihilates, with its fiery heat, all objects in its pathway, so rushed the angry soldiery from room to room, ruthlessly destroying all that was within their reach. Furniture, pianos, books, manuscripts; in short, everything in the house was flung out of the windows, while wardrobes and other articles too heavy to move were first cut up with hatchets, and the legs of pianos sawn off. These two houses were in the best quarter of the town, and occupied only by well-to do people. An idea may be formed of the quantity of furniture they contained from the fact, that there were from fifteen to twenty pianos.

When the brutal and insensate soldiery arrived at the second storey of the house inhabited by Chopin's sister, the mementoes of the great artist, which the whole family cherished with such pious care, were doomed to destruction. The piano—one of Buchholtz's—on which he had received his earliest instruction, and which had been the confidant and interpreter of his first musical ideas, was flung into the street by these Vandals.* At night

---

* The Pleyel piano sent from Scotland in 1858, was fortunately in the possession of Chopin's niece, Madame Ciechomska, who lived in the country.

the soldiers made a stack of the ruined furniture
in the square at the foot of the statue of Copernicus,
and filling their kettles with the wine, spirit, and
sugar from the ransacked shops, they made merry
round the fire, mixing punch and singing boisterous
songs. Pictures, books, and papers—among the
latter Chopin's correspondence with his family
during eighteen years—were thrown in to feed the
flames. Eye-witnesses relate that an officer, having
lighted upon a portrait of Chopin, painted by a
friend, gazed at it long and earnestly before committing his wanton deed. The reflection which
illumined the city anounced to the terrified inhabitants that the reign of military terror had begun.

But more to be deplored than the loss of any other
relics, is the destruction of the letters, in which
Chopin had poured forth all his affection for his
family, his love for his country, his enthusiasm for
his art, and his admiration for all that is beautiful
and noble. The letters to his parents from Paris,
written at a period when he was daily gathering
fresh laurels, and was in intimate relations with
the leading artists and the highest personages in
the State, were not only of extreme interest, but
of historical value, as faithful and vivid pictures
of the times. For in these spirited and witty
writings, Chopin often gave, in a word or two, a
more life-like portrayal of his contemporaries than
is to be found in many a long and elaborate description. The brightest, happiest period of his life, its

real summer-time, was between the years 1832 and
1837; while his sojourn in Vienna, with all its hopes
and dreams, may be called the spring-time of his
existence.    But the non-fulfilment of these hopes
depressed the readily despondent spirit of the artist.
The delicacy of his constitution, and the nervous
excitability induced by constant pianoforte playing,
unfortunately deprived him of that energy, of which
no one is more in need than the musician who performs in public. Chopin succumbed to instead of
fighting against difficulties; he loved peace; but
life—and to the artist above all—is a battle.

Being a stranger in Vienna, he was obliged to
depend on the advice of others, and was alternately
suspicious and mistrustful, or confiding as a child.
The disturbances in his country deprived him, as
a Pole, of the protection of the chief, dignitaries
of Vienna; while among the artists he met with
indifference, and sometimes envy.    Thus, irreso-
lute, and dispirited, he beheld other pianists gaining
profit and approbation, and himself only took part in,
a single matinée given on April 4th, in the large
Redoubt Hall, by the vocalist, Madame Garcia-
Vestris.  He gave but one concert,* and that not

---

* There is a notice of this concert, probably by Kandler, in
No. 38 of the *Allgemeine Musikalische Zeitung* for September
21st, 1831.  It says, "Frederic Chopin, whose visit, last year,
showed him to be a pianist of the first rank, has given a
concert here.  The performance of his new Concerto, which is
of an earnest character, gave us no occasion to alter our first

until the beginning of June, when, according to
their annual custom, and partly also on account of
the cholera epidemic, the wealthier inhabitants had
left the city; as might be expected the attendance
was small, and the expenses exceeded the receipts.

Disappointed in his expectations, Chopin went to
Münich, where he was obliged to stay some weeks,
awaiting money for his journey to Paris.   This gave
him an opportunity of becoming acquainted with the
first artists : among others, Bärmann, Berg, Shunke,
and Stunz, who, delighted with his playing and his
works, persuaded him to perform at the Philharmonic
Society's concerts.    At one of these Frederic played
his E minor Concerto, with orchestral accompaniments.    Carried away alike by the beauty of the
composition, and the charm and poetry of the
execution, the audience overwhelmed the young,
*virtuoso* with hearty and genuine applause.

This was Chopin's swan-song on German soil, for,
during the eighteen years of his residence abroad, he
never again publicly performed in Germany.    His
last visit to Vienna seemed to check all his desires
in that direction.

Encouraged by his success in Münich, Chopin left
that hospitable town for Stuttgart, where a heavy

---

opinion. So sincere a worshipper of true art is worthy of all
honour."   Other Vienna journals spoke in the same manner of
his compositions, and praised his skilful and expressive playing;
but these acknowledgments did not satisfy the hopes and
wishes of the young artist.

trial awaited him: the news of the capture of
Warsaw by the Russians, September 8th, 1831.
Grief, anxiety, and despair as to the fate of his
family and his beloved one filled up the measure of
his misery.   Under the influence of these feelings he
wrote, while still at Stuttgart, the magnificent C
Minor Study, (the last in the first collection, dedicated
to Liszt) frequently called the "Revolutions-Etude."
Amid the wild storm of rushing passages in the left
hand the melody rises, now passionately, now in
proud majesty, bringing to the mind of the thrilled
listener the image of Zeus hurling his thunderbolts
at the world.

In such a mood Chopin left for Paris at the end
of September, 1831.   His passport bore the words,
"passant par Paris à Londres;" and, years after,
when he had become domiciled and naturalised in
France, he often said, with a smile, "I am only
passing through."

With this concludes the information kindly afforded
me by the Chopin family.   I must now have recourse to my own recollections to Chopin's letters,
and to the narrations of trustworthy witnesses who
were in communication with him either by letter
or in person during his residence in the French
capital.

# CHAPTER XIII.

WHEN Chopin came to Paris, it was stirred by a
considerable amount of political agitation;
despite all the efforts of the Legitimists, as the
partisans of Charles X. and his descendants were
called, Louis Philippe, by favour of the barricades,
reigned on the ruins of the Bourbon dynasty. As
we have said, things had not yet quieted down,
and every section of the populace was divided into
parties. Although not advantageous to art, the political situation was of little consequence to Frederic,
as he had gone to Paris, not for the sake of performing in public, but solely for self-improvement.

Soon after the taking of Warsaw the Polish army
retired into Prussia and Austria, and many of its

members found their way to Paris, the fugitives receiving a hearty welcome as they passed through Germany.* All who, whether in politics or in the field, had been foremost in the revolution—the members of the diet, officers, poets, and writers, who by patriotic songs or newspaper articles had incited the people to insurrection—were in dread of the vengeance of Russia, and took refuge in France, hoping that, sooner or later, her sympathy with the wrongs suffered by Poland would move her to their redress. Miserable delusion! terrible were its consequences! Thousands of intelligent men left the country, carrying with them the light they had shed on science and art, while their loss, as Russia saw with satisfaction, was irreparable, for none were found worthy to take their place. Years of sad experience were needed to convince the Poles that their expectations were foolish, their efforts for freedom useless, and their hopes for aid from France futile.

Chopin, of course, soon became the centre of the Polish emigrants in Paris. Assured about the safety of his relatives in Warsaw, his spirits improved, and he would often ask himself, "What shall my future be?" The plans of his tour, which he had formed at home, having been utterly thwarted, he was

---

* Leipsic was foremost in this. Many German poets also expressed their sympathy with the oppressed Polish nation in spirited songs.

obliged to start afresh. To give a concert in Paris did not seem practicable, for who would be likely to take any interest in a young, unknown pianist, because he had the effrontery to perform in public? The few words of praise in the Vienna and Leipsic papers made no impression in Paris, where the public were busy with politics and amusements of all kinds. Besides, the musical world there set little or no store on _critiques_ in foreign newspapers. Paris, they thought, was the oracle for the whole civilized world, and only on the banks of the Seine was a European reputation to be made or marred. Frederic was anxious not to let slip the precious opportunity. He considered himself far from being a perfect artist, and, therefore, resolved once more to seek instruction from Kalkbrenner.

Frederic Kalkbrenner, then at the height of his fame as a _virtuoso_, was regarded as the first pianist in Europe. Chopin, therefore, paid him a visit, and expressed his desire of becoming his pupil. Directly the young Pole began to play, Kalkbrenner perceived his genius, and that he had nothing more to learn. Chopin, with his modesty and zeal after the highest attainments in art, little imagined what was passing in Kalkbrenner's mind. To the latter's fame as a pianist nothing could add, but he might also attain the reputation of a first-rate teacher, were he to obtain a pupil of such rare gifts as Chopin. He, therefore, thought it wise not to refuse to take him. Kalkbrenner, whose judgment was authoritative, and who either thought his own opinions infallible or knew how to proclaim them as such, fancied he could pick holes in Chopin's playing; he declared that his fingering was quite opposed to the classic method; that his execution was not that of the best school; that he was indeed a gifted *virtuoso* and composer, but that, although on the right road, he might easily go astray.

Chopin listened in silence, while M. Kalkbrenner announced that he was ready to give him lessons, that he might cure him of those faults which would always be a hindrance to his progress, but only on condition that Chopin promised to remain with him for at least three years. The young artist was much surprised at such a stipulation, but, not yet fully conscious of his own worth, he determined to pause before deciding on a matter of such supreme importance to him. He, therefore, wrote to his father, and to Elsner, to ascertain their wishes and opinions. Elsner was not a little astonished at Kalkbrenner's request, and inquired why such a long discipline was required for a pianist like Chopin; did Kalkbrenner desire to undo what was already done, and to destroy Chopin's originality? Elsner knew better than anyone else what a deep spring of originality lay hid in the mind of Chopin, and to what degree his technical powers were developed. Accordingly he was in favour of cultivating Chopin's "virtuosity," with a view to his career as a composer, rather than of hindering the free development

of his creative power by a one-sided musical training.
He expressed these opinions in the following letter to
his beloved pupil :—

"*Warsaw, November 27th,* 1831.

DEAR FREDERIC,

I was pleased to see, by your letter, that Kalkbrenner, the first of pianists, as you call him, gave
you such a friendly reception.   I knew his father, in
Paris, in 1805; and the son, who was then very
young, had already distinguished himself as a first-
rate *virtuoso.*   I am very glad that he has agreed to
initiate you into the mysteries of art, but it astonishes
me to hear that he requires three years to do so.
Did he think the first time he saw and heard you,
that you needed all that time to accustom yourself to
his method ?  or that you wished to devote your
musical talents to the piano alone, and to confine
your compositions to that instrument ?  If he, with
his artistic experience, desires to render service to
our art in general, and to you in particular, and if
he shows himself your sincere friend, then be to him
a grateful pupil.

"In the study of composition, a teacher ought not
to be too narrow-minded and particular, especially
with pupils of decided talent, and who display a
certain independence of invention.   They should
rather be allowed to go their own way, and to make
new discoveries.   The pupil must not only stand on
the same artistic platform as his master, but, when

possessing pre-eminent talent, must rise beyond it, and so cultivate his abilities as to shine by his own light.

" The playing of any instrument—be it ever so perfect, like that of Paganni on the violin, or Kalkbrenner on the piano—is, with all its charm, only the means, not the end of the tone-art. The achievements of Mozart and Beethoven as pianists have long been forgotten, and their pianoforte compositions, although undoubtedly classic works, must give way to the diversified, artistic treatment of that instrument by the modern school. But their other works, not written for one particular instrument, the operas, symphonies, quartets, &c., will not only continue to live, but will, perhaps, remain unequalled by anything in the present day. ' Sapienti pauca.'

" A pupil should not be kept too long to the study of one method, or of the taste of one nation. What is truly beautiful must not be imitated, but *felt*, and assimilated with the individual genius. The only perfect nature is the Divine, and art must not take one man, or one nation as a model, for these only afford examples more or less imperfect. In a word, that quality in an artist, (who continually learns from what is around him) which excites the wonder of his contemporaries, can only arrive at perfection by and through itself. The cause of his fame, whether in the present or the future, is none other than his own gifted individuality manifested in his works.

" More bye and bye. Please remember me kindly

to Count Plater, Grzymala, Hofmann, Lesueur, Päer, Kalkbrenner, and Norblin. Embrace Orlowski for me.

JOSEPH ELSNER."

To these weighty observations Frederic sent the following reply :—

*Paris, December* 14*th*, 1831.

DEAR MONSIEUR ELSNER,

Your letter gave me a fresh proof of your fatherly care and sincere interest in me, your grateful pupil. At the beginning of last year, although fully conscious of my deficiencies, and of how far I was from attaining to the model which I had set before myself in you, I ventured to think that I could follow in your footsteps, and that I might produce, if not a Lokietek, perhaps a Laskonogi.* But now all those hopes have vanished; I have to think how I can best make my way as a pianist, and so must, for a time, leave in the back ground the loftier artistic aims of which you spoke.

To be a great composer, it is not only needful to possess creative power, but experience and the capacity for self-examination, which, as you have taught me, is not acquired by the mere hearing of

---

* Lokietek and Laskonogi were Kings of Poland, and so called, the former on account of his small size, the latter because he had spindle legs. Elsner wrote an opera, in 1818, entitled " Lokietek," which was very successful.

P

other people's works, but by a careful criticism of one's own.

Many young and very talented pupils of the Parisian Conservatoire are waiting with their hands in their pockets for the performance of their operas, symphonies, and cantatas, which hitherto only Lesueur and Cherubini have seen on paper. I am not speaking of the smaller theatres, although these are difficult enough of approach. And when, like Thos. Nidecki, at the Leopoldstädter Theatre in Vienna, a composer is fortunate enough to obtain a performance, he reaps but little benefit from it, even when, as in this case, the work is a good one. Meyerbeer, too, after he had been famous in the musical world for ten years, stayed three years in Paris waiting, working, and spending money, before he succeeded in bringing out his "Robert le Diable," which has now made such a *furore*. Auber, with his very popular works, had forestalled Meyerbeer, and was not very ready to make room at the Grand Opera for the foreigner.

In my opinion, the composer who can perform his works himself is best off.

I have been recognised as a pianist at two or three cities in Germany; several of the musical papers gave me commendatory notices, and expressed a hope that I should soon take a prominent position among the first pianoforte *virtuosi*. Now that I have an opportunity of fulfilling my self-made promise, should I not embrace it? I did not care to study pianoforte playing in Germany, for no one could tell me exactly what I was deficient in. Neither did I see the beam in my own eye. Three years of study is a great deal too much, as Kalkbrenner himself perceived when he had heard me two or three times. From this you can see, dear Mons. Elsner, that the true *virtuoso* does not know what envy is. I could make up my mind to study three years, if I felt certain that would secure the end I have in view. One thing is quite clear to my mind; I will never be a copy of Kalkbrenner; he shall not destroy my bold, it may be, but noble resolution of creating a new era in art. If I take any more lessons now it will only be that I may become independent in the future. Ries, when he had gained a name as a pianist, found it easy to win laurels in Berlin, Frankfort-on-the-Maine and Dresden as the composer of " Die Räuberbraut ;" and what a number of years Spohr, had been a famous violinist before he wrote " Faust," " Jessonda," &c.! I trust you will not withhold your sanction when you see with what aims and on what principles I am acting.

No doubt my parents have told you that my concert is fixed for the twenty-fifth of this month. The preparations have given me a great deal of trouble, and had not Päer, Kalkbrenner, and especially Norblin, (who sends kindest regards to you), taken the matter in hand, I should have been helpless. Just imagine, it takes at least two months to get up a concert in Paris. Baillot is exceedingly kind; he offered to play a Quintet of Beethoven's with me, and Kalkbrenner a duet with an accompaniment of four pianos. Mons. Reicha I only know by sight, and you can guess how curious I am to become personally acquainted with him. Those of his pupils whom I have seen gave me no very favourable account of him. He does not like music, and will not talk about it; he never goes to the Conservatoire concerts, and when he gives lessons he looks at the clock all the time. Cherubini acts in a similar fashion, and talks of nothing but cholera and revolution. These masters are like mummies, to be respectfully regarded at, a distance, while one draws instruction from their works.

Fétis, whose acquaintance I have made, and from whom much may be learned, only comes to Paris to give lessons. It is said that he does so from necessity, as his debts exceed the profits of the *Revue Musicale*. He is in danger sometimes of seeing the inside of the debtor's prison. But, as in Paris, a debtor can only be legally arrested in his own house, Fétis has left the city for the suburbs; Heaven knows where!

There are a host of interesting people here belonging to the various professions. Three of the orchestras can be called first-rate: that of the Academy, the Italian Opera, and the Théâtre Feydeau.

Rossini is director of the Italian Opera, which is undoubtedly now the best in Europe. Lablache,

Rubini, Santini, Pasta, Malibran, and Shröder-Devrient perform three times a week for the delectation of the *élite*. Nourrit, Levasseur, Derivis, M^me. Damoreau-Cinti, and M^lle. Dorus are the stars of the Grand Opera. Choliet and M^lle. Casimir Prévost are much admired at the Comic Opera; in a word, only in Paris can one learn what singing really is. I believe that Malibran-Garcia, not Pasta, is now the greatest songstress in Europe. Prince Valentin Radziwill is quite captivated by her, and we often wish you were here, for you would be charmed with her singing.

Lesueur thanks you for your kind remembrances, and commissions me to return them a thousand-fold. He always speaks of you in a friendly way, and asks every time I see him: " et que fait notre bon Mons. Elsner? Racontez-moi de ses nouvelles;" and then speaks of the Requiem you sent him. Everybody here, from your god-son the young Anton Orlowski to myself, loves and esteems you. I fear our dear friend will have to wait some time for the performance of his opera. The subject is nothing particular and the theatre is closed till the new year.

The King is not very free with his money, the artists need a great deal, and the English are the only people who pay well. I could go on writing till to-morrow, but will not put your patience to such a test. Believe me, with all respect and gratitude,

Ever your faithful pupil,

FREDERIC.

Not only Elsner's letter, and the advice of friends, but his own sound understanding made Chopin feel how superfluous and even ignominious such a course of lessons would be. He justly perceived that he must either become a servile copy of Kalkbrenner, or soon cease to be his pupil ; and that as he had been able to maintain his artistic independence beside Field and Hummel, he could not do better than give up Kalkbrenner's instruction and take his own way. To preserve his friendly relations with Kalkbrenner, and from a genuing feeling of esteem, he dedicated to him his E minor Concerto. Chopin writes to his friend Titus Woyciechowski * at this time :—

Paris, December 6th, 1831.

MY DEAR TITUS,

Your letter gave me new life. I receive such contrary reports, some of which make me very anxious, for I often put a wrong construction on what my family write. K. expressed himself so strangely, that I was frightened at my own thoughts when I read his words. I trust we may see each other again in this life. I have been greatly pained by all that has happened. Who could have foreseen it ?† Have you forgotten our deliberations the night before your departure from Vienna ? Fate has sent

---

* This friend says that the later letters, from Paris, are all lost, with the exception of two little notes written in the year of Chopin's death, the last he wrote to Woyciechowski.

† The Polish Revolution.

me hither where I can breathe freely . . . . . But this is a cause of trouble.

In Paris you find everything. You can amuse yourself, weary yourself, laugh, weep, and above all, do what you like, without a soul taking any notice of you, because thousands are doing likewise. Everybody goes his own way. I believe there are more , pianists, more *virtuosi*, and more donkeys in Paris than anywhere. I came here, as perhaps you have heard, with very few introductions. Malfatti had given me a letter to Päer, I received two or three from the Viennese publishers: and that was all. When the news of the capture of Warsaw reached me at Stuttgart, I determined to go to Paris. Through the band-master Päer, I have become acquainted with Rossini, Cherubini, Baillot, and Kalkbrenner.

You can imagine how eager I was to hear Herz and Hiller play; but they are nothing to Kalkbrenner. To tell the truth, I can play as well as Herz; I wish I could say as well as Kalkbrenner, who is perfection in quite another style to Paganini. Kalkbrenner's fascinating touch, the quietness and equality of his playing, are indescribable; every note proclaims the master. He is truly a giant, who dwarfs all other artists. When I presented myself to Kalkbrenner he asked me to play something. What could I do? However, having heard Herz, I plucked up my courage, and played my E minor Concerto, which took so immensely in the Bavarian

capital.  Kalkbrenner was astonished, and asked if
I were a pupil of Field.  He remarked that I had
Cramer's style, but Field's touch.  I was very much
amused by Kalkbrenner, who, in playing to me,
made a mistake which brought him to a stand-still;
but the way in which he recovered himself was
marvellous.  Since this meeting we have seen each
other every day; either he comes to me, or I go to
him.  He offered to take me as a pupil for three
years, and to make a great artist of me.  I replied
that I knew very well what were my deficiencies;
but I did not wish to imitate him, and that three
years were too much for me.  He has persuaded me
that I only play well when I feel inspired.  The
same cannot be said of him, for he plays one time
just like another.  After watching me for some time,
he said that I belonged to no school, that although I
was undoubtedly progressing very well, I might
easily go astray, and that when he left off playing
there would be no representative of the great pianoforte school.  Further, that however much I might
have the will, I could never create a new school, for
I was not acquainted with the old ones.  But I am
certain that there is an individuality about my compositions, and I shall always strive to go forward.

If you were here I know you would say : "learn,
young man, as long as you are told to."  But many
friends advise me not to take lessons; they think that
I play as well as Kalkbrenner, and that he only
wants to have me as a pupil out of vanity.  That

is absurd. Anybody who understands music must appreciate Kalkbrenner's talents, although he is personally unpopular, as he will not associate with everybody. But I can assure you there is something superior about him, as about all the *virtuosi* whom I have hitherto heard. I told my parents so, and they quite understood it, but Elsner did not; he considered that Kalkbrenner found fault with my playing out of jealousy. Nevertheless, I have already made a name among the artists here.

I am going to give a concert on the 25th of December, with the assistance of Baillot, Paganini's rival, and Brod, the celebrated hautbois player. I am going to play my F minor Concerto, and the variations in B major. Of the latter, I received from Cassel, a few days ago, a review, ten pages long, by an enthusiastic German, who, after an exhaustive preface, analyzed every bar. He does not consider them variations according to the orthodox style, but a picture of the imagination. He says of the second variation that Don Juan and Leporello are running; of the third that he is fondling Zerline to the disgust of Masetto. In the D flat major in the fifth bar of the Adagio he can perceive Don Juan kissing Zerline. A comical conceit of the reviewer's, who is very anxious that the composition should be printed in the *Revue Musicale* (a paper belonging to his son-in-law Fétis.)

The good Hiller, a very talented young man, and a pupil of Hummel, gave a concert the day before

yesterday, which produced a great effect. One of
his own symphonies was received with loud applause.
He has made Beethoven his model, and his work is
full of poetry and enthusiasm. He was sufficiently
interested in me to tell Fétis's father-in-law that he
would do me more harm than good by that notice of
his. But to return to my concert : I am not only to
play the F minor Concerto and the variations, but
perform, with Kalkbrenner, his duet, " Marche
suivie d'une Polonaise," for two pianos, with accompaniments for four pianos. Is not that a wild
idea ? One of the pianos is very large and is for
Kalkbrenner, another very small one (a so-called
monochord) is intended for me. On the other large
ones, which make as much noise as an orchestra,
Hiller, Osborne, Stamaty, and Sowinski are to play.
Norblin, Vidal, and the famous viola player, Urhan,
will also assist. The most difficult matter of all
was to find a vocalist. Rossini would willingly have
helped me to obtain one if he had been allowed to,
but Robert, the second director of the Italian Opera,
objected. He declared that if it were known he
had obliged me he should be besieged by hundreds of
similar applications.

As to the opera, I must say I never heard such a
fine performance as last week, when the " Barbiere "
was given, with Lablache, Rubini, and Malibran-
Garcia. There was, too, an excellent rendering of
" Otello," with Rubini, Lablache, and Pasta ; also
the " Italiana Algeri." Paris has, in this respect,

never offered so many attractions as now. You can have no idea of Lablache. They say that Pasta's voice has rather gone off, but I never in my life heard such heavenly singing as her's. Malibran's wonderful voice has a compass of three octaves, and she is in her style unique and fascinating. Rubini, a capital tenor, makes no end of *roulades*, and often too many *coloratures*, but by his incessant recourse to the trill and *tremolo*, he wins enormous applause. His mezza-voce is incomparable. A certain Schröder-Devrient has just come out, but she does not make such a *furore* here as in Germany. Signora Malibran gave " Otello ;" Schröder-Devrient, Desdemona. Malibran is a much smaller woman than the German singer, and people thought, several times, that Desdemona would strangle Othello. This was a very expensive performance. I paid twenty-four francs for my place, just to see Malibran as the Moor, and not a very extraordinary impersonation either. The orchestra was first-rate, but the appointments of the Italian-Opera are nothing to those of " L'Académie Royale."

I do not believe that any spectacle at the Italian Opera, however brilliant, ever came up to that of " Robert le Diable," the new five-act opera of Meyerbeer, the author of the " Crociato." " Robert " is a master-piece of the new school, in which devils sing through speaking trumpets, and the dead rise from their tombs, but not as in " Szarlatan," * only fifty

---

* An opera by Kurpinski, performed with great success in Warsaw.

or sixty at once. The stage represents the interior of a ruined cloister, with the moonlight falling brightly on the nuns lying in their graves. In the last act monks appear with incense amid a gorgeous illumination, and the solemn strains of the organ re- sound from the adjacent building. Meyerbeer has, by this work, made himself immortal; yet it took him more than three years to obtain a performance of it. It is said that for the organ and other accessories he paid more than twenty thousand francs.

Madame Damereau-Cinti is also a very fine singer; I prefer her to Malibran. The latter astonishes, but Cinti fascinates you. She sings the chromatic scales and *coloratures* almost more perfectly than the famous flautist, Tulou, plays them. It would be almost impossible to find a more perfect *technique*. Nourrit, the first tenor at the Grand Opera, is admired for his warmth of feeling. Chollet, the first tenor of the Opera Comique, the best impersonator of Fra Diavolo and excellent in the operas "*Zampa*" and "Fiancée," has quite an original manner of conceiving a part. He charms universally by his sympathetic voice, and is the darling of the public. The "Marquise de Brinvilliers" is now being played at the Opera Comique; this marquise was the most famous poisoner in the time of Louis XIV. The music is by eight composers: Cherubini, Päer, Herold, Auber, Berton, Batton, Blangini, and Caraffa.

I pray, above all, dear Titus, that you will write to me soon, or come yourself. My address is,

Boulevard Poissonnière, 27. W. W. expects you. I should be so delighted to see you, and there are times when I am almost mad with longing, especially when it rains, and I cannot go out. I shall, I think, have the assistance of the best artists at my concert.

Yours till death,

FREDERIC.

------

We see from this letter that Chopin was delighted with Paris. He found himself highly esteemed by the most celebrated artists, yet much still remained for him to desire. He had come to Paris with very modest means, and with neither fame nor patronage, but he did not wish to be always dependent on the kindness of his father, who was far from rich, and had daughters to care for. Much, too, as Frederic liked France, especially Paris, he felt that he was in a foreign country, and that the Poles with whom he associated were fugitives. It gave him pain to hear his native land mentioned. Under these circumstances, he curtailed his expenditure as much as possible, and shared his lodgings with needy friends.

He had hoped that his concert would make him a name among the musical public, but as the theatrical director, Véron, would not permit any of his singers to assist, the performance was of necessity postponed till February 26th, 1832. Unfortunately, however, the receipts did not even clear

the expenses, for only the well-to-do among the
Polish refugees attended, and there was scarcely
a French person present. Chopin's friends tried
to console him by telling him of the difficulties other
artists had had to struggle against in their early days.
His true friends—and he had indeed some such—
advised him to go more into society, for which he
had plenty of opportunity, but on this point he
was not to be persuaded. The letters to his parents
at this period are tinged with melancholy.

His stay in Paris was saddened by the absence
of any prospect of improving his position. He,
therefore, turned his thoughts to quite another plan
of life. Some young Polish exiles, who were neither
able nor willing to remain in Paris, had resolved
to go to America. Chopin, knowing there was a
lack of good artists in the New World, thought
that he should do well to go there, and so be
no longer a burden to his father. He knew
full well that his parents expected his entire confidence, so he communicated his intentions, endeavouring to persuade them that he could do nothing
better than leave France, and seek his fortunes on
the other side of the Western ocean.

One involuntarily asks: what part could be played
by Chopin, with his romantic and poetical nature,
in a country where coolness and practical ability are
of paramount importance? With his life-long horror
of charlatanism, his refined taste and aristocratic
tendencies, how could he have lived in America,

or how could the Americans have appreciated him?
Had he settled there merely as a teacher, he would,
perhaps, have grown rich; but he would never have
shone among the stars of the musical world.

Fortunately for Chopin his parents were thoroughly
opposed to his emigrating. They conjured him to
stay in Paris and wait for brighter days, or to return
to Warsaw. Rather than consent to his going to
America, they would endure to see their son exposed
to the disagreeable consequences imposed by the
Russian Government on every one who remained
abroad after his passport had expired. His love
for his country, his family, and one whose image
was deeply seated in his heart, awakened an ardent
longing to return home, although it was not easy
for him to leave Paris with its manifold attractions.
His friends and fellow-artists, Franz Liszt, Hiller,
and Sowinski, tried to dissuade him from leaving
Paris, but Chopin would not listen to them.

His meeting with Prince Valentine Radziwill in
the street on the very day that Chopin was preparing
for his departure, may appear to many persons as
mere chance, but it was not unlike a Providential
arrangement. The Prince was very friendly, and
Chopin divulged his intention, and bade him farewell. Instead of venturing to dissuade him from
his purpose, the Prince exacted a promise that he
would spend the evening with him at Rothschild's.
In after life the importance of that evening often
recurred to Chopin.

In the brilliant *salons* of the financial king, the artist, whose every hope had fled, met the *haute volée* of Paris. The hostess asked him, in a kind manner, to play something, and he played and improvised as he had, perhaps, never done before. His audience were enraptured; they vied with each other in expressing their respect and admiration, and were unwearied in praising his talents. From that evening his position changed as if by magic; the future once more smiled upon him, the mists which had hidden the sunshine of his life disappeared before the bright rays of his rising fortunes. Even during the *soirée* Chopin received several requests to give lessons from the first families in Paris. His pecuniary affairs improved daily. There was no further occasion for him to take anything from his parents, and he entirely gave up the idea of returning to Warsaw.

# CHAPTER XIV.

COINCIDENT with the rise of Chopin's star above the horizon of Parisian society was the spread of his fame as a composer, so that after 1832 his works, some of which he had written in his own country, some in Vienna, Leipsic, Paris, or during his travels, became widely diffused. They included the three Nocturnes, op. 15; Bolero, op. 19; Scherzo, op. 20; Grande Polonàise Brillante, op. 22; Ballade, op. 23; four Mazurkas, op. 24; two Polonaises, op. 26; two Nocturnes, op. 27; and Impromptu, op. 29.

By most of the professional critics, these were, as we have already said, dogmatically condemned as being devoid of all artistic merit. There were, however, some few—but very few indeed—who unreservedly recognized the boldness and originality of thought, the rare wealth of harmony, and the newness of form displayed in Chopin's compositions, and

who were not staggered by the novelty of a fingering, totally opposed to the traditional method.
Field and Moscheles, however, could not forgive
Chopin's frequent departures from the customary
and classical forms, nor could they regard him as
other than a bold revolutionist. In 1833 Moscheles
wrote on Chopin's early works as follows : *

"I gladly avail myself of a few leisure evening hours
to become acquainted with Chopin's Etudes and other
works. Their originality and the national colouring of
the motives are very charming ; but my fingers are
constantly stumbling over hard, inartistic, and to me
incomprehensible modulations, so that the whole often
seems too cloying, and unworthy of a man and an accomplished musician."

Later on he writes :—

"I am a sincere admirer of Chopin's originality ; he
produces the newest and most attractive pianoforte work.
But personally, I object to his artificial and often forced
modulations ; my fingers stick and stumble at such
passages, and practise them as I may, I never play them
fluently."

Although he somewhat modified this opinion in
after years, it is indicative of the impression produced on the most celebrated pianists by Chopin's
early works. Field had a presentiment that his own
glory would be dimmed by the rise of this new and

---

* See Moscheles's Life.

brilliant orb, and he publicly spoke of Chopin as,
"un talent de chambre de malade." This criticism,
which principally found credence in Germany, was
for ever silenced by the pen of Eusebius and
Florestan, in Robert Schumann's *Neue Zeitschrift
für Musik.*

The fame and popularity of Chopin in the Paris
*salons* increased with marvellous rapidity. He was
overwhelmed with requests to play at public concerts,
for it was well-known how attractive he was to
cultivated audiences. On May 20th, 1832, he played
at a concert in the hall of the Conservatoire, got up
by the Prince of the Muscovites for the benefit of the
poor. He chose the first Allegro from his F minor
Concerto with orchestral accompaniments,* Girard
directing. Heinrich Herz asked Chopin and Liszt
to take part with him in a quartet for eight hands on
two pianos, at a concert he wished to give with his
brother Jacob, on April 3rd, 1833. Orlowski, a
fellow student of Chopin's, wrote to his own family
about that time :—

"Chopin is healthy and strong; he turns the heads of
all the ladies, and the men are jealous of him. He is
now the *mode*, and the fashionable world will soon be
wearing gloves à la Chopin. But he pines after his
country."

---

* This work was first performed in England at one of the
trials for the King's Scholarship, at the Royal Academy of
Music.—*Translator's Note.*

Johannes Matuszynski, who came to Paris in the same year (1834) to study medicine, says the same thing in a letter to his father-in-law, in Warsaw :—

" The first thing I did, on-arriving in Paris, was to find out Chopin, and I cannot describe what a pleasure it was to us both to meet again after an absence of five years.   He has grown so strong and big that I scarcely knew him again.   Chopin is the first pianist in Paris, and gives a great many lessons, but none under twenty francs.   He has composed a great deal, and his works are very much sought after.   I am living with him in the Rue Chaussée d'Antin, No. 5.   This street is indeed rather far from the School of Medicine and the hospitals ; but I have good reasons for wishing to be with him ;   he is all in all to me.   We spend the evening at the theatre or in visiting, and if we do neither of these we make our-selves comfortable at home."

Elsner followed from a distance the artistic de-velopment of his beloved pupil, with the warmest interest, and rejoiced over his success.   He wrote to him as follows :—

*Warsaw, September 14th, 1834.*

Everything that I hear and read about my dear Frederic gives me pleasure, but pardon my candour when I say that I have not yet heard enough to satisfy me, whose pleasure it was, unworthy as I am, to be your teacher in harmony and counterpoint, and who will ever be one of your best friends and admirers.   Before I leave *hac lacrimarum valle* I should like to see a per-formance of your operas, not only for the sake of increasing your fame, but in the interests of musical art generally, especially if the subject were taken from the history of Poland. I am not saying too much. You know that I cannot flatter you, as I am acquainted not only with your genius but with your capacities, and I know that what the critic referred to in your Mazurkas will only become valuable and lasting in an opera.*

Urban says, " that a pianoforte composition stands in the same relation to a vocal, orchestral, or a composition for any other instrument, as an engraving does to an oil painting." This is sound criticism, although some compositions (especially when you play them) may be regarded as coloured plates.

What a pity it is that we can no longer see and talk to each other; I have a great deal more that I could tell you. And I want also to thank you for the present, which is doubly valuable to me. I wish I were a bird that I might visit you in your Olympian abode, which the Parisians consider a swallow's nest.

Farewell; love me as I love you, for I am now and ever

Your sincere friend and well-wisher,

JOSEPH ELSNER.

---

* The author says, in a note, that he does not know to what critique or to which Mazurkas Elsner refers. There are eight sets of these "cabinet pictures," as Liszt calls them, and, as one of Chopin's most enthusiastic critics remarks, they vividly pourtray his patriotic and home feelings. He calls them green spots in the desert, quaint snatches of melancholy song, outpourings of an unworldly and trustful soul, musical floods of tears and gushes of pure joyfulness.—*Translator's Note.*

Elsner's letter made Chopin think seriously about composing an opera, and he asked his friend Stanislas Kozmian to write a libretto on a subject from Polish history. Unfortunately, however, either from want of time, or because he feared the Russian Government might object to a Polish national opera, Frederic soon relinquished the idea. Perhaps also the approbation and popularity which his pianoforte works met with everywhere, and especially in Paris, induced him to adhere to that kind of composition. In February, 1834, he gave his second public concert in Paris. It took place at the Italian opera-house, and was the most brilliant performance of the season. Habeneck conducted, and the Concerto in E minor was performed for the first time.

Everything seemed to promise the most satisfactory results for the *bénéficaire*. The hall was filled with the best of the Parisian aristocracy, with whom Chopin was the first favourite, and the presence of the foremost artists gave an especial interest to the event. But Frederic's hopes were disappointed. His refined and poetical playing could not be heard to advantage in the large theatre; and it failed to arouse the enthusiasm of the audience. Chopin felt this, and for a long time was unwilling to play again in a large public hall. The *salon* and a select circle of poets, artists, and connoisseurs formed a more fitting arena for the triumphs of the gifted and keenly sensitive artist.

Like those rare and beautiful plants which can

only flourish in a soft genial climate, Frederic, with
his exquisite culture and delicate sensibilities, could
only play *con amore* when in the best society, and
among connoisseurs who knew how to appreciate
all the niceties of his performance, which under such
conditions had a truly magical charm. It was not
in Chopin's nature to win the favour of the general
public; and we might say of him, in Goethe's words:

> " Wer den Besten seiner Zeit genug gethan,
>     Der hat gelebt fur alle Zeiten !"

With the exception of a journey to Rouen, to
take part in his friend Orlowski's concert, which
was a great sacrifice in the cause of friendship, as
appearing in public was distasteful to him, Frederic
made no more artistic tours after he settled in Paris.
He said in confidence to Liszt : " I am not adapted
for giving concerts : I feel timid in the presence
of the public; their breath stifles me, their curious
gaze paralyzes me; but with you it is a vocation, for
if you do not please the public you know how to
agitate and confound them."

But in the midst of a circle of beautiful women,
surrounded by friendly and familiar faces, a new
poetical life stirred within him; the look of melancholy, which so often overshadowed his face, yielded
to an amiable and sympathetic smile; the earnest
and beautiful expression of his features was wonderfully fascinating; his conversation sparkled with
intelligence, and, unconsciously to himself, the

influence of his fresh and harmless wit was in-
describably felt by those around. When in a happy
mood, his improvisation delighted and elevated the
minds of his hearers, or if he happened to be under
the inspiration of Comus,* awakened a sense of the
purest and most innocent joy. He was often in
those moods in French, but more often in Polish
households, in which, of course, he felt more at
home, and, although in the midst of Paris, could
fancy himself once more in his beloved fatherland.

He liked to have all the new *belles lettres* publica-
tions sent to him. To any poem that took his fancy
he would write a melody, which was soon spread
abroad by his friends Fontana and Orda. (The
latter, a youth of great promise, fell in Algiers).
Prince Casimir Lubomirski, Grzymala, and other
musical Poles took an interest in these improvisations, and helped to make them known. These
songs were often heard at the houses of Countess
Komar, and her charming daughters—one of whom
was Princess Beauvau—where Chopin was always
a welcome guest. The clever Princess and her
younger sister, the Countess Delphine Potocka,
famous for her rare beauty and her fascinating
singing, gathered around them the *élite* of the literary
and artistic world. No wonder was it that the

---

* The God of festive mirth is represented in the Greek
mythology as a winged youth.

young Countess made a profound and striking impression on the susceptible heart of Frederic, and that it was a delight to him to accompany her magnificent voice with his poetical playing.

In the latter half of May, 1834, Chopin determined, for the first time, to forsake his pupils and take a trip to Aix-la-Chapelle, with Ferdinand Hiller, in order to be present at the grand Lower-Rhine musical festival, conducted by Mendelssohn. Chopin's friendship with the celebrated composer of " St. Paul " dated from their meeting in Paris, in 1832, and resting as it did on mutual regard, was now confirmed and strengthened. Mendelssohn, who was at that time director of the Düsseldorf Stadt Orchestra, was much pleased to meet, at Aix-la-Chapelle, his old friend Hiller, and also Chopin, whose compositions he esteemed very highly. During the festival he spent as much time as possible with the two Parisians, about whom he wrote, on May 23rd, to his mother :—

" They have both made progress in their playing, and Chopin is now one of the first pianists ; he produces as many novelties on the piano as Paganini does on his violin, and marvels that one would not have thought possible. Hiller, too, is an excellent player, with plenty of force and fancy. But both of them aim rather at Parisian sensationalism, and too often disregard time, repose, and true musical feeling. I, perhaps, incline to the opposite extreme, and so we supplied each other's deficiencies, and all three, I believe, learnt something from one another. About me there was a dash of the school-master, about them the *soupçon* of a *mirliflore* or an *incroyable*. After the festival we travelled together to Düsseldorf, and spent a very pleasant day in music and discussion; yesterday, I accompanied them to Cologne; and early this morning they went up by steamer to Coblentz, and I came down. Thus ended the charm-ing episode." *

A great pleasure was in prospect for Chopin in the following year. His father had been strongly urged by the Warsaw doctors to go to Carlsbad for the sake of his health, and as soon as Frederic heard that this was decided on he left Paris, about the end of July, and in a few days had the pleasure of embracing his beloved parents, whom, for five years, he had so painfully missed. It is more easy to imagine than to describe the delight of this meeting. Their dear little Frederic had become a man, and had grown stronger and more staid. He had acquired a certain dignity of bearing, which well became him, and which commanded the respect of the artistic world; but in affection and gratitude to his parents he was the same Fritz, who in child-hood and youth had delighted the hearts of his father and mother. The time sped very enjoyably, and the sad and trying parting hour came a great deal too soon for Frederic no less than for his affectionate father and tender mother. Again and

* "Mendelssohn's Letters." Second Series.

again they clasped their beloved son in their arms,
vainly endeavouring to banish the presentiment that
they would never see him again in this world.  And
this was the last time that these good parents,
whose constant care was for the welfare of their son,
ever beheld him.

Frederic spent a few days at Leipsic on his return
to Paris.   His arrival had been expected, and of
course there was a great excitement in artistic
circles about the playing of so original and poetic
a composer.  The conflicting opinions about his
works added to the interest of his visit.  A letter
from Frederic Wieck, father of the famous Clara,
to Nauenburg, a music teacher at Halle, shows
what a sensation the coming of Chopin created
among the musicians of Leipsic.*   It runs as
follows :—

"DEAREST FRIEND,

I hasten to answer your letter of the 19th, which I
received last evening.   Banck returns to-morrow, so
then we shall be altogether.   Now for the musical news.
The first subscription concert, under the direction of
Mendelssohn, will take place on October 4th, the second
on the 11th.  To-morrow, or the next day, Chopin will
arrive from Dresden, but probably he will not give a
concert, for he is very lazy.  He might have remained

---

* This letter bears no date, but was probably written about
the end of September, 1835.  It is to be found in the autograph
collection of Hermann Scholtz, at Dresden.

longer here, had he not been dissuaded by a false friend
(a dog of a Pole) from making the acquaintance of the
musical world of Leipsic; Mendelssohn, however, who
is very friendly with Schumann and myself, will perform. According to a speech which Chopin made to a
friend in Dresden he does not believe there is a lady in
Germany who can play his compositions. We will see
what Clara can do."

There seems to me no justification for the ill-
humour of the much-esteemed musical pedagogue,
who is so uncomplimentary in his expressions and
so hasty about the imaginary false friend. Chopin
had not thought of giving a concert in Leipsic, as he
was only passing through, and he had, moreover, a
great dislike to performing in public. He was very
pleased with the Leipsic artists, and played some of
his own compositions to them at Mendelssohn's
house; he also heard Clara Wieck, and was delighted
with her poetical playing, and, astonished at the
marvellous attainments of one so young, for whom
he prophesied a brilliant future

It is quite possible that Chopin may have doubted
whether there was a lady in Germany capable of
playing his compositions; but it is very unlikely
that he should have said so, for he was always very
gallant to ladies, and was, as we know, a sincere
admirer of Fräulein Blahetka's playing.

In a letter from Mendelssohn to his sister Fanny
Henselt, we find the following :—

*Leipsic, Oct. 6th,* 1835.

. . . . . The day after I left Henselt's for Delitzsch Chopin arrived there; he could only stay a day, so we spent the whole of it together and had music. I cannot help saying, dear Fanny, that I have recently discovered that your criticism did not do him justice; perhaps, as is often the case, he was not in the right humour when you heard him. I have once more been charmed by his playing, and I am convinced that if you and father had heard him perform some of his best compositions as he played them to me, you would say the same thing.

There is something so thoroughly original and masterly about his pianoforte playing, that he may be called a truly perfect *virtuoso ;* and as I love perfection in any form, I spent a most agreeable, although a very different day from that with you at Henselt's. I was very glad to be once more with a thorough musician, not with those half *virtuosi* and half classists, who would like to unite in music " les honneurs de la vertu et les plaisirs du vice," but with one who has a clearly defined aim, and although this may be the poles asunder from mine, I can get on with such a person capitally, but not with those half-and-half people. Sunday evening was really very remarkable when Chopin made me play over my oratorio to him, while curious Leipzigers stole into the room to see him, and when, between the first and second parts, he dashed into his new *études* and a new Concerto, to the amazement of the Leipzigers; and then I resumed my " St. Paul." It was just as if a Cherokee and a Kaffir had met to converse.

He also played a sweetly pretty new nocturne, a good deal of which I have got by heart that I may please Paul by playing it to him. Thus we had a good time of it together, and he promised faithfully to return in the winter if I would compose a new symphony and give a performance of it in his honour; we pledged ourselves, in the presence of three witnesses, so we shall see whether we both keep our word.

This letter shows that Mendelssohn had no great antipathy to Chopin's compositions, and that he was much interested by many of them; Mademoiselle Ehlert, the authoress of "Musical Letters to a Friend," is, therefore, wrong in placing Mendelssohn among Chopin's opponents. It has been said that Mendelssohn would not allow his pupils to play Chopin's compositions. As far as I know, the composer of "St. Paul" and "Elijah" had no time to give lessons, and it is quite understandable that he may not have recommended Chopin's works to the pupils of the Leipsic Conservatoire. But, with his love of justice, Mendelssohn felt it his duty to combat the objections of his sister, who had been educated on the old classic principles.

Chopin's second and last sojourn in Germany was in 1836. Under the pretext of trying a cure he went to Marienbad, and there his destiny was decided. Every flame, however fierce, must expire unless it receive nourishment. Constantia Gladkowska, whom the youthful Frederic had worshipped as a saint, married in Warsaw. When Chopin heard the news he was deeply grieved and even angry. But time, which heals all wounds, calmed his passionate spirit.

Chopin met in Paris some young. Poles of good family—the brothers Wodzynski, who had been at his father's *pension*. Through them he became acquainted with their sister Maria, a charming and amiable girl. He felt attracted towards her at first sight, and his interest gradually changed to ardent love. Knowing that in the middle of July she would be with her mother at Marienbad he went thither, full of hope and longing. Chopin soon discovered that Maria returned his affection, and they were engaged with the glad consent of their relatives. When they left Marienbad the Wodzynski family decided to spend a few weeks with Chopin at Dresden.

Frederic felt at this time at the topmost pinnacle of happiness, and his gay humour communicated itself to everyone around him. His friends, remembering the harmless but clever jokes he used to play in his youth during his visits to the country, rejoiced that the famous artist, the darling of Parisian drawing rooms, had so preserved his natural simplicity and loveable modesty. They would laughingly recall how often he used to take his sisters' delicate evening gloves when he could not afford to buy new ones for himself, and how he promised to send them gloves from Paris by the dozen; a promise which, as soon as he had made a position in that city, he conscientiously performed.

He would often mimic the playing of the most celebrated European *virtuosi*, imitating them even in the minutest details.   He frequently played his mazurkas, which are full of a sweet melancholy, and then show how the rhythm must be shortened to adapt them for dancing.   Directly the conversation turned upon his own family he grew serious ; he was no longer the artist indulging his own wayward fancies, but the grateful son and affectionate brother.   From infancy till death he had constantly received proofs of the tenderest affection, and his glowing and sensitive heart was bound to his parents and sisters by innumerable and indissoluble ties ; he therefore suffered more from absence than many another.

When full of the hope of becoming a happy bridegroom, he formed a plan for leaving Paris, his second home, with all its fascinating charms, its glittering *salons*, the scene of so many of his triumphs, and returning to Poland.   He wished to withdraw from the world and to settle in the country near his family in the neighbourhood of Warsaw ; there he would establish schools for the people, and, without troubling himself about the public, quietly pursue his beloved art.   With this idea in his mind, he bade, as he thought, a short adieu to his bethrothed, and set off for Paris through Leipsic.

Frederic wrote to Robert Schumann, who, having long desired to make his acquaintance, looked anxiously forward to his arrival.   Chopin on his side was very pleased to have a chance of becoming acquainted with and personally expressing his regard for so famous a man. It was about this meeting that Schumann wrote the following letter to the Chapel-master, Heinrich Dorn :—

*Leipsic, September, 6th, 1836.**

MY VERY DEAR SIR,

The day before yesterday, just as I had received your letter and was about to answer it, who should walk in but Chopin. This was a great pleasure to me, and we spent a delightful day together . . . . . . I have got a new *ballade* of his; it seems to me the most pleasing but not the cleverest of his works (genialischtes nicht genialstes werk.) I told him I liked it best of all, and after a long pause he said, with much emphasis, " I am very glad you do, for it is my favourite also."

He played also a host of new studies, nocturnes and mazurkas, all of them inimitable. The way in which he sits down to the piano is exceedingly impressive. You would be very pleased with his playing; yet Clara is a greater *virtuosa* than even he. Imagine to yourself perfection unconscious of its own merit.

Pleased with the warm reception of the German artist Chopin quitted Leipsic after having cast a garland on the monument of Prince Joseph Poniatowski.†

---

* " Eine Biographie," von Joseph Wilhelm von Wasietewski, Dresden, 1869.

† In what was formerly called the Reichenbach, but now the Gerhard Gardens, there is a monument of Prince Ponialowski, who was drowned in the Elster, October 19th, 1813.

R

He was very busy with his own thoughts; he believed that his wandering life was now ended, and that with his new duties he would enter on a new career. Thinking of his lovely bride he soared on the rosy wings of fancy into an ideal land amidst images of indescribable happiness and blessed hope.

Rough reality, alas! aroused him from his delicious dreams, and inflicted a deep and painful wound upon his heart. Some time after his return to Paris, he learned that his bride had elected to marry a count instead of an artist. The consequences to Chopin were very serious: finding that his hopes of an ideal union were shattered, to wipe out and forget the insult he had received, he threw himself into the arms of a woman who exercised a very pernicious influence over him.

# CHAPTER XV.

*CHOPIN'S ACQUAINTANCE WITH GEORGE SAND.*
*HIS LIFE AMONG HIS FRIENDS. WINTER SOJOURN*
*IN THE ISLAND OF MAJORCA (1838-1839.)*

IT had been raining the whole day, and Chopin, whose nerves were painfully affected by changes of weather and especially by damp, was in wretched spirits. None of his friends had been in to see him, there were no new books to amuse or excite him, and no melodious thoughts demanding expression had presented themselves. At length, when it was nearly ten o'clock, it occurred to him to go to Countess C.'s, who had her *jour fixe*, when an intellectual and agreeable circle always assembled in her *salon*. As he walked up the carpeted steps Chopin imagined himself followed by a shadow, exhaling an odour of violets; he had a feeling that he was in the presence of something strange and wonderful, and felt almost inclined to turn back; then, laughing at his superstitiousness, he sprang lightly up the remaining steps and entered the room. A numerous company was assembled, and,

See Mcc v.

mingled with the well-known faces, there were some that he had not seen before.

The party had broken up into groups, talking, with French grace and vivacity, of the theatre, literature, politics and the events of the day. In a humour for listening rather than talking, Chopin sat down in a corner of the room and watched the beautiful forms passing before him, for many charming women frequented Countess C.'s.

When part of the company had gone and only the intimate friends of the hostess remained, Chopin, who was in the mood for weaving musical fairy tales, (Märchen) sat down to the piano and improvised. His hearers, whom in his absorption he had quite forgotten, listened breathlessly. When he had finished he looked up, and saw a simply dressed lady leaning on the instrument and looking at him with her dark passionate eyes as if she would read his soul. Chopin felt himself blushing under her fascinating gaze; she smiled slightly, and when he retired behind a group of camelias he heard the rustling of a silk dress, and perceived the odour of violets. The lady who had looked at him so inquiringly while he was at the piano was approaching with Liszt. In a deep musical voice she said a few words about his playing, and then spoke about the subject of his improvisation. Frederic felt moved and flattered. Undoubtedly the highest reward of the poet and artist is to find themselves understood; and while listening to the sparkling intellectual eloquence and poetry of her words, Chopin felt that he was appreciated as he had never been before. This lady was Aurora Dudevant, at that time the most celebrated of French authoresses, whose romances, written under the name of George Sand, were, of course, well known to him. That night, when he returned home, the pleasing words were still ringing in his ears, the flashing glance was still dazzling his eyes. But this first interview impressed his intellect only ; his heart and his sense of beauty were untouched. He wrote to his parents, "I have made the acquaintance of an important celebrity, Madame Dudevant, well-known as George Sand ; but I do not like her face, there is something in it that repels me." But when he met this talented woman again, her attractive conversation, in which was nearly always hidden some delicate flattery, made him forget that she was not beautiful. Her love for him—for George Sand was passionately enamoured of Chopin—gave to her decided and rather manly features a certain attractive softness, and made her shy and almost humble towards him ; thus, unconsciously, she stirred his heart. Frederic felt at first merely grateful to her ; then, if not as passionately, yet truly and deeply he returned her love. The wound inflicted by Maria's faithlessness was healed. The consciousness of being loved by the foremost of French authoresses, a woman of European celebrity, filled Frederic with happy pride. He was no longer alone and solitary, for Aurora Dudevant was not only his beloved, one, but an intellectual and steadfast friend in whose heart he found a home from which fate could never banish him.

He began about this time to withdraw from large assemblies, and spent most of his time in communion with his muse, and among a small circle of friends. Always fastidious about his surroundings, he was even more so now ; but he always received his intimate acquaintances with perfect good humour and true Chopin amiability. Franz Liszt, Ferdinand Hiller, and Baron von Stockhausen are, perhaps, the only living representatives of those interesting "soirées intimes" at Chopin's house in the Rue Chaussée d'Antin. Liszt writes :—

" His apartment was only lighted by some wax candles, grouped round one of Pleyel's pianos, which he particularly liked for their slightly veiled yet silvery sonorousness, and easy touch, permitting him to elicit tones which one might think proceeded from one of those harmonicas of which romantic Germany has preserved the monopoly, and which were so ingeniously constructed by its ancient masters from the union of crystal and water.

" As the corners of the room were left in obscurity, all idea of limit was lost, so that there seemed no boundary save the darkness of space. Some tall piece of furniture, with its white cover, would reveal itself in the dim light ; an indistinct form, raising itself like a spectre to listen to the sounds by which it had been evoked. The light concentrated round the piano glided wave-like along the floor mingling with the red flashes of fire-light.

A solitary portrait, that of a pianist, a sympathetic friend and admirer, seemed invited to be the constant auditor of those sighing, murmuring, moaning tones which ebbed and flowed upon the instrument. By a strange accident, the polished surface of the mirror reflected, so as to double for our eyes, the beautiful oval with the silky curls which has so often been copied and of which countless engravings have been reproduced for the friends of the elegant composer."

Among the frequent guests at this abode were: Heinrich Heine, the German poet, of whom Enault said that sarcasm had consumed his heart, and scepticism swallowed up his soul; Meyerbeer, the greatest dramatic musician of the day; Liszt, who astonished the world with his magnificent impassioned playing, and who, understanding the poetic soul of the Polish artist, paid a literary tribute in after years to his memory; Ferdinand Hiller,* a famous pianist and a warm and faithful friend of Chopin; Ary Schäffer, the most classic of the Romantic painters; Eugène Delacroix, who sought for harmony of colour in Chopin's enchanting music; Adolphe Nourrit, the celebrated singer, who, under the influence of melancholy, committed suicide;(?) Baron von Stockhausen, ambassador of the King of Hanover at the French court, a pupil and

---

* Hiller wrote some beautiful verses full of deep feeling for the festival in memory of Chopin, held at Düsseldorf, November 3rd, 1849.

admirer of Chopin; and besides these, a little
band of his own countrymen, at whose head was
the veteran Niemcewicz, who had such an ardent
yearning for his fatherland that his one wish was to
rest from his labours in his native soil; Mickiewicz,
the greatest of Polish poets, who, ever dreaming
of his beloved Lithuania, celebrated its beauty in
verse worthy of a Homer; the favourite poet
Witwicki; Matuszynski, Fontana, Erzymala, and
last of all Musset's " la femmé à l'œil sombre,"
who empoisoned the later life of our artist, so that
he might have said with a bleeding heart as Musset
did, " et si je ne crois plus aux larmes, c'est que je
l'ai vu pleurer." Only those who had seen Chopin
receiving these friends and gracefully dispensing true
Polish hospitality, and who had also been fortunate
enough to hear him improvise, could say that they
really knew him. The confidential talk of a small
circle would put him in the best of humours, and
he would often be as merry as in the early happy
days of youth in his father's house, before he had
become acquainted with the cares and troubles of
life.

Chopin was not fond of giving up his time to
others, but when he did, he did so entirely. If an
old friend or fellow-student from Warsaw came to
see him, he would immediately put off his pupils
and devote the day to his visitor. He would then
order a carriage, take his guest to breakfast on the
Boulevards, and drive around the suburbs (generally

to Montmorency). After some hours of innocent enjoyment in the country, they would return to Paris, dine at one of the best restaurants, and finish the day at the theatre. After that they would occasionally go to some tea-garden or pleasure "local," where there would be no lack of amusement and pretty dancers. On such occasion Frederic was the Amphytrion of his guests, and would never suffer them to pay anything. This kind of Parisian life could not but be injurious to Chopin's delicate constitution. In the Autumn of 1837 * he had, for the first time, a pulmonary attack which much weakened him. Both his friends and the physicians were very anxious about his health; it was generally thought that he was in consumption, and he was urged to go to the South of France. Just at that time George Sand was intending to go to the Island of Majorca for the sake of her son Maurice, and pressed Chopin to go with her. Frederic found it very hard to leave Paris, and to separate himself from his doctor, his friends, and his piano. He was by disposition loth to break up pleasant associations, and every change agitated him, but he could not say no to a woman whom he so revered.

His friends did not think this journey at all advisable; Frederic was not, however, very much exhausted by it, but as soon as he landed, in November, 1838,

---

* In the same year Chopin paid a short visit to London in company with Camillo Pleyel and Stanislas Kozmian, senior.

he was taken dangerously ill. The cold and damp of his first apartments gave him a violent cough, and the new-comers were regarded with such evident dislike by the occupants that they hastened to quit the house. In Majorca, consumption was thought as infectious as cholera and the plague, and no one would take in the invalid. At length he and his friends found shelter in a very lonely and slightly built house (karthaus) called " Waldemosa," which had just been vacated by the monks. This cloister was situated in a charming glen, surrounded by orange trees; but, of course, in such a building there was not a trace of comfort, and it did not contain a particle of furniture. The winter that year was a very hard one; it rained for a fortnight without ceasing, and snow fell several times. Chopin, therefore, sent to Marseilles for a stove and a piano; but, as he said in writing to his parents, he was obliged to wait for them a long time. When at length they arrived the authorities and inhabitants of Palma were in a great state of excitement; they regarded these strange objects as diabolical machines intended to blow up the town.

Our artist did not receive the wished for benefit from his stay in Majorca, but grew paler and thinner every day. Although his complaint was anything but chronic, all the doctors gave up attending him. Chopin himself was perfectly composed about his condition. The last physician whom he had consulted, not thoroughly understanding

his disease, did not use the right means to arrest
it, and the bronchitis was followed by a nervous
agitation, which the doctor, not having observed
the contrary symptoms, treated as phthisis. He
ordered stimulating diet, bleeding, and a milk cure.
These measures were quite opposed to the nature of
the complaint. The effects of the loss of blood were
almost fatal, and Frederic's sufferings increased
daily. The doctor constantly insisted on bleeding,
but the friend, who nursed him with the utmost care,
seemed to hear a voice saying, " it is killing him."
It soon appeared that this was a Providential presentiment. The milk cure did not succeed; there
were no cows in the neighbourhood, and Frederic
did not like that which was substituted—goat's
milk.

" The poor great artist! It was difficult sometimes
to know how to treat him," says George Sand.*
" What I feared, unhappily came to pass—he lost all
patience. He bore his bodily sufferings like a man, but
he could not bridle his ever restless imagination. The
house seemed to him full of spirits—spectres which
plagued him more than his pulmonary pains. He tried
to hide from us what was troubling him, but we soon
found it out. Coming back, one evening, about ten
o'clock with my children from visiting the ruins of the
cloister, we found Chopin at the piano. His looks were
wild, his hair stood on end, and it was some seconds

---

* " Histoire de ma vie." Vol. III. chap. 6 and 7.

before he recognized us. Then he forced a smile and began to play something. During the short time he had been left alone, in his depression, a host of demoniacal thoughts had, against his will, crowded upon him.

"While staying in this ' card house,' he composed some short but very beautiful pieces, which he modestly entitled ' Preludes;' they were real master-pieces. Some of them create such vivid impressions that the shades of the dead monks seem to rise and pass before the hearer in solemn and gloomy funereal pomp.* Others are full of charm and melancholy glowing with the sparkling fire of enthusiasm, breathing with the hope of restored health. The laughter of children at play, the distant strains of the guitar, the twitter of the birds on the damp branches, or the sight of the little pale roses in our cloister garden, pushing their heads up through the snow, would call forth from his soul melodies of indescribable sweetness and grace. But many also are so full of gloom and sadness that, in spite of the pleasure they afford, the listener is filled with pain.

" I apply this especially to a Prelude † he wrote one evening, which thrills one almost to despair. One day Maurice and I went to Palma to make some necessary purchases. Chopin was pretty well when we left him. Towards evening a heavy rain set in; the rivers swelled rapidly; we lost our boots in the floods; our driver deserted us; and we were exposed to great danger. It was with difficulty that we accomplished a mile and a

---

* The middle movement, for example, of No. 15 in D flat major.

† No. 6, B minor.

half in six hours, and we did not reach home till midnight. We were greatly vexed at arriving so late, as we
knew our dear invalid would be very uneasy. We found
him, indeed, in a state of great agitation, and already
beginning to despair. With tears in his eyes he had
composed this noble and beautiful Prelude. When he
saw us come in, he jumped up with a cry, stood almost
motionless, and in a strange, hollow voice, exclaimed:
" Ah, I thought you were dead ! " By degrees he grew
calm, but when he saw our soaked and ruined clothes,
the thought of the danger to which we had been exposed
again unnerved him. He told us afterwards that during
our absence he had had a vision, and that he could not
distinguish the dream from the reality. He had sunk
into a kind of stupor and fancied, while he was playing,
that he had been removed from earth, and was no longer
in the land of the living. He imagined that he was
drowned, and as he lay at the bottom of the sea could
feel the cold drops keeping time as they dropped upon
his breast. When I called his attention to the even fall
of the rain upon the roof, he obstinately maintained that
he had not heard it before.

" He was vexed with me for using the expression,
' harmonie imitative,' and he was right, for imitation is
an absurdity which can only tickle the ear. There was
in Chopin's genius a subtle innate harmony which
reflected the expression of his musical thoughts by a
lofty assonance of tone, not through the material repeti-
tion of the outward sound. The Prelude he wrote that
evening recalls, indeed, the rain drops falling on the
roof of the cloister, but according to his conception these
drops are tears falling from heaven on his heart.

" As yet, no other genius has appeared so full of deep
poetic feeling as Chopin. Under his hand the piano
spoke an immortal longing. A short piece of scarcely
half a page will contain the most sublime poetry.
Chopin's rich genius never needed the aid of gross
material means. No! He required no trumpets and
ophicleides to awaken terror or enthusiasm. Hitherto
he has not been understood, and even now is not
generally appreciated. Musical taste and feeling must
make considerable progress before Chopin's works can
be popular.

" Chopin felt both his power and his weakness; the
latter arose from an excess of power which he did not
know how to control. He could not, like Mozart—who
in this capacity stands alone—create master-pieces from
common-place tones. Chopin's compositions contain
many surprises and *nuances* which are often strange,
mysterious, and original; but never far-fetched or
strained. Although he hated and avoided what was
incomprehensible, the over-intensity of his feelings
often carried him into regions to which he only
could attain.

" I fear that I was often a bad judge; for he was in
the habit of asking me for advice, as Molière did his
cook; and when I had come to know him intimately his
style was quite clear to me. During the eight years
in which I became increasingly familiar with his musical
thoughts, and had acquired an insight into his character,
I used to find in his playing either an exaltation, a
struggle and a victory, or else the agony of an over-
mastering thought. At that time I understood him
as he understood himself; a critic who knew him less

intimately would perhaps have advised him to express himself more clearly.

" In youth he was full of witty and merry thoughts, as some simple yet exquisite Polish songs give evidence. Some of his later tone-poems bring before us a sparkling, crystal stream reflecting the sunbeams. Chopin's quieter compositions remind us of the song of the lark as it lightly soars into the æther, or the gentle gliding of the swan over the smooth mirror of the waters; they seemed filled with the holy calm of nature. When Chopin was in a desponding mood the piercing cry of the hungry eagle among the crags of Majorca, the mournful wailing of the storm, and the stern immoveability of the snow-clad heights, would awaken gloomy fancies in his soul. Then, again, the perfume of the orange blossoms, the vine, bending to the earth beneath its rich burden, the peasant singing his Moorish songs in the fields, would fill him with delight.

" Chopin's character thus showed itself in varying circumstances; although sensitive to all marks of friend-ship and smiles of favour, he would remember the slightest offence for days and weeks together. The most trivial *contre-temps* would disturb him exceedingly ; but, what is still more strange, real grief never troubled him so much as small vexations. He could not overcome this weakness of character, and his irritation was often out of all proportion to the cause. He bore his illness with heroic calm and courage; real dangers did not frighten him, but, like very imaginative and nervous men, he would torment himself ceaselessly with melancholy thoughts.

" His excessive anxiety about trifles, his insuperable

repugnance to the slightest sign of poverty, and his luxurious habits, must have made his residence in Majorca, after some days of illness, very distasteful to him. But he was not in a condition to travel; and when at last he had somewhat recovered, contrary winds arose and the ship was obliged to lie at anchor for three weeks. It was our only means of return, and unfortunately we were not able to avail ourselves of it. Our stay at the Cloister was a misery to Chopin and a hard trial to me. His agreeableness and cheerful amiability in society were frequently matched by the gloominess and peevishness of his behaviour to those around him at home, whom he sometimes drove almost to despair. Yet I never knew anyone so noble-minded, tender, and free from selfishness. He was a faithful and honest friend. In happy moments his brilliant wit often surpassed the cleverest sayings of the most eminent men; and on matters which he thoroughly understood the soundness of his judgment was incomparable. On the other hand, you would rarely meet with a man of such exhaustless imagination and such a strange and irritable disposition. But who could quarrel with the talented artist for the waywardness and peculiarities that were the results of ill health? A broken rosebud, the shadow of a passing chafer affected him as much as if he had been bled or touched with glowing iron.

" The only objects he cared for were me and my children; everything else in the South seem unbearable to him. His impatience at the delay of our departure did him more harm than all his vexation over the want of comfort. Finally, at the latter end of the winter we were able to go to Barcelona and from thence to Marseilles."

When they landed at this city Chopin learnt that a funeral mass was to be performed for the celebrated singer, Adolphe Nourrit,* who in a fit of insanity had committed suicide. Frederic immediately hurried into the church, and during the service seated himself at the organ and played his last improvisation in honour of his departed friend.

---

* Adolphe Nourrit, the greatest tenor of his day, born at Montpelier, March 3rd, 1802, threw himself out of a window, in Naples, March 3rd, 1839, because he fancied he was not receiving so much applause as formerly.

## CHAPTER XVI.

*RETURN TO PARIS. MOSCHELES AND LISZT.*
*CHOPIN AS A PIANOFORTE TEACHER.*

AFTER spending a fine summer at Nohant, the
country residence of George Sand, Chopin
returned to Paris in the autumn. His health and
spirits had been excellent during the whole time,
and if not perfectly restored he was yet sufficiently
strong to resume his usual occupations. It appeared
that the doctors had been mistaken; what they took
for consumption turned out to be bronchitis; they,
therefore, strongly advised the artist to spare his
strength as much as possible and lead a very regular
life.

A tender mother or sister, or a loving and beloved
wife, would doubtless have succeeded in inducing
Frederic, who was naturally gentle and tractable, to
pay more regard to the delicacy of his constitution
and pursue quieter habits; but in Paris, where he
spent every evening at assemblies which lasted late
on into the night, he could not make up his mind to
stay at home and go to bed early. This exciting life

was very injurious to him; the first symptoms of consumption appeared, and increased in severity year by year.

Chopin lived first in the Rue Tronchet, but he soon moved to the Quai d'Orleans, where he occupied the "pavilion" of a house inhabited by George Sand. "Chopin was very pleased to have a drawing room in which he could play and dream; but he was very fond of society, and used it chiefly to give lessons in," says George Sand; "it was only while he was at Nohant that he composed." His pupils welcomed him back with great pleasure, and were charmed with the preludes and the host of new compositions which he brought with him.*

In 1839 Moscheles, who had been desirous of knowing the Polish *virtuoso*, arrived in Paris from London. The two artists met for the first time at an evening party at the house of Monsieur Leo, to whom Chopin dedicated the Polonaise, op. 53. As polished men of the world, they saluted each other with the utmost courtesy, but went no further. After this first brief meeting they were both invited by King Louis Philippe to a concert at St. Cloud, on November 29th.

Chopin played before the royal family a nocturne and some studies, and was, as Moscheles says,

---

* These compositions are: second impromptu, op. 36; two nocturnes, op. 37; scherzo (C sharp minor), op. 39; two polonaises, op. 40; four mazurkas, op. 41; valse, op. 42; tarantelle, op. 43; &c., &c.

" admired and petted as a favourite." The German
artist then played some drawing-room pieces, and, in
conclusion, his Duet Sonata, with Chopin. Moscheles
thought Chopin's playing full of charm and life, and
in a letter to his wife he says :—

" Chopin's appearance corresponds exactly with his
music; both are delicate and fanciful (schwärmerisch.)
He played to me at my request, and then for the first
time I really understood his music and saw the explana-
tion of the ladies' enthusiasm. The *ad libitum* which
with his interpreters degenerates into bad time, is, when
he himself performs, the most charming originality of
execution; the harsh and dilettante-like modulations,
which I could never get over when playing his compositions, ceased to offend when his delicate fairy-like
fingers glided over them; his *piano* is so delicate that
no very strong *forte* is required to give the desired
contrast. Thus we do not miss the orchestral effects
which the German school demands from a pianist, but
feel ourselves carried away as by a singer who, paying
little heed to the accompaniment, abandons himself to
his feelings. He is quite unique in the pianistic world.
He declared he liked my music very much; at any rate
he is well acquainted with it. He played his Studies,
and his last new work, the ' Preludes,' and I played
several of my works to him. Who would have thought
that, with all his sentimentality, Chopin had also a comic
vein ? He was lively, merry, and extremely comic in
his mimicry of Pixis, Liszt, and a hunch-backed pianoforte amateur."

Chopin's imitative talent displayed itself, as the

reader knows, in early youth, and increased so much in after years that the French players, Boccage and Madame Dorval, declared that they had never seen anything of the kind so excellent before. My friend, Joseph Nowakowski, a fellow-student of Chopin, relates the following anecdotes :—

"When I visited Chopin in Paris, I asked him to introduce me to Kalkbrenner, Liszt, and Pixis. 'That is unnecessary,' answered Chopin; 'wait a moment, and I will present them to you, but each separately.' Then he sat down to the piano after the fashion of Liszt, played in his style and imitated all his movements to the life; after which he impersonated Pixis. The next evening I went to the theatre with Chopin. He left his box for a short time, and turning round I saw Pixis beside me. I thought it was Chopin, and I laughingly clapped him on the shoulder, exclaiming, leave off your mimicry. My neighbour was quite flabergasted by such familiarity on the part of a total stranger, but fortunately at that moment Chopin returned to the box, and we had a hearty laugh over the comical mistake. Then, with his own peculiar grace of manner, he apologized both for himself and me to the real Pixis.

"Liszt frequently met Chopin in society and had many opportunities of observing his imitative talent. He looked quietly on while Chopin mimicked him, and, far from being offended, he laughed and seemed really amused by it. There was not the slightest jealousy between these two artists, and their friendship remained unbroken.

"One day Chopin was asked at a party to play some

of his latest works, and Liszt joined in the request. On sitting down to the piano, Chopin noticed that there were no pedals, and the hostess then remembered that they had been sent away for repair and had not been brought back. Liszt laughingly declared that he would furnish them himself, and crawling under the piano he knelt there while Chopin played, and completely supplied the place of the pedals.*

"Some years afterwards, in June, 1843, a large number of artists were assembled at Nohant. Among them were Liszt, the celebrated Pauline Viardot-Garcia, whose incomparable power of ideal expression made her the best interpreter of Chopin's Polish songs; the painter, Eugène Delacroix, many of the best actors and several eminent literary people. The hostess, with her son and daughter and some married couples from the neighbourhood, completed the party, all of whom were young enough to be enthusiastic about art, and full of hope.

"One evening, when they were all assembled in the *salon*, Liszt played one of Chopin's nocturnes, to which he took the liberty of adding some embellishments. Chopin's delicate intellectual face, which still bore the traces of recent illness, looked disturbed; at last he could not control himself any longer, and in that tone of *sang froid* which he sometimes assumed he said, ' I beg you, my dear friend, when you do me the honour of playing my compositions, to play them as they are

---

* Chopin relates this in a letter to his parents, which I myself read, but which, unfortunately, is among those that were destroyed.

written or else not at all.' ' Play it yourself then,' said
Liszt, rising from the piano, rather piqued. ' With
pleasure,' answered Chopin. At that moment a moth
fell into the lamp and extinguished it. They were going
to light it again when Chopin cried, ' No, put out all the
lamps, the moonlight is quite enough.' Then he began
to improvise and played for nearly an hour. And what
an improvisation it was! Description would be impossible, for the feelings awakened by Chopin's magic
fingers are not transferable into words.

" When he left the piano his audience were in tears;
Liszt was deeply affected, and said to Chopin, as he
embraced him, ' Yes, my friend, you were right; works
like yours ought not to be meddled with; other people's
alterations only spoil them. You are a true poet.' ' Oh,
it is nothing,' returned Chopin, gaily, ' We have each
our own style; that is all the difference between us.
You know, quite well, that nobody can play Beethoven
and Weber like you. Do play the Adagio from Beethoven's C sharp minor Sonata, but nicely, as you can
do when you choose.' Liszt began his Adagio, his
hearers were moved deeply, but in quite another manner.
They wept, but not tears of such sweetness as Chopin
had caused them to shed. Liszt's playing was less
elegiac, but more dramatic."

" Some days afterwards," writes Charles Rollinat, in
*Le Temps*, " We were once more the guests of George
Sand. Liszt asked Chopin to play, and, after a little
pressure, he consented. Liszt then desired the lights to
be put out and the curtains drawn that it might be
perfectly dark. This was done, and just as Chopin was
sitting down to the piano Liszt whispered something to

him and took his place. Chopin seated himself in the nearest arm chair, not dreaming of his friend's intention. Liszt immediately began to improvise in the same manner as Chopin had done on the former evening, and so faithfully copied both sentiment and style that the deception was perfect. The same signs of emotion were again perceptible among the audience, and just as the feeling reached its height Liszt lighted the candles on the piano. A general cry of astonishment echoed through the room. ' What, it is you ? ' ' As you see,' said Liszt, with a laugh. ' But we made sure it was Chopin playing,' rejoined the company. In this ingenious way Liszt revenged himself on his dangerous rival.

" Comedies were sometimes performed, or improvised recitations delivered, the latter spontaneous and poetical, as all true improvisations ought to be. There was a theatre in George Sand's chateau, and also a great variety of costumes. Only the subject of the piece and the number of scenes needed to be given ; the actors improvised the dialogue. Liszt and Chopin were the orchestra ; they sat at two pianos right and left of the stage behind some drapery, and followed the play with appropriate music.

" Both artists were endowed with an astonishing memory. They had at their command all the Italian, French, and German operas of importance, and could select, with marvellous readiness, motives adapted to the particular situation, and work them out so effectively and with such fervour that the actors—whose own achievements were by no means inconsiderable—called out from the stage, ' Hold, you are too lavish with your beauties.'

" In the middle of the garden was an esplanade, commanding a view of the whole valley. A table, some stone benches, and a light garden seat seemed to invite the loiterer to stay and rest. The esplanade was surrounded by a strong iron railing, to prevent the children who played there from falling into the brook. The spot was noted for a wonderful echo, which repeated every word three or four times with perfect clearness. The children often amused themselves in what they called making the echo talk. One evening the thought occurred to somebody of bringing out the piano and letting the echo repeat fragments of romantic music. The idea met with universal approval, and the magnificent Erard Instrument was taken out on to the esplanade.

" It was a clear, still night in June; there was no moon, but in the place of her silvery light shone a countless host of stars. The piano was opened towards the valley, and Liszt's energetic hands performed the well-known hunting chorus from 'Euryanthe.' He stopped, of course, to wait for the echo after each pause. Even after the first we were all wild with enthusiasm; there was something marvellously poetic in nature thus echoing art. The musical phrase was too long both the first and second time for the echo to give it back clearly; but the third and fourth time the echo of the echo in the chorus was beautifully repeated, without missing a note, by the natural echo. Liszt himself felt the spell and quickened the time. Every phrase excited the liveliest curiosity and the most intense expectancy. One in particular swept with a sweet melancholy sound over the tops of the trees in the valley; but the last announced the triumph of the human will over the obstacles opposed by nature.

" After this most artistically managed Fanfare, Chopin took Liszt's place and made the echo sing and weep. He played some scraps' from an impromptu which he was at that time composing. Frederic's delight over this diaphanous Æolian music knew no bounds; he continued his converse with the spirits of the valley much longer than Liszt had; it was a strange communion, a whispering and a murmuring like a magic incantation.

" The hostess was almost obliged to draw him by force from the piano; he was in a state of feverish excitement. When Chopin had finished playing, Pauline Garcia sang the lovely naïve romance, ' Nel cor piu non mi sento.' It was an excellent choice, for every phrase consisted of only two notes, which, to the intense delight of us all, the echo repeated with astonishing clearness. Aurora had already begun 'to spread her rosy veil before the party broke up, carrying with them not only a delicious impression but, doubtless, an undying recollection."

As is so often the case in life, the warm friendship between Liszt and Chopin grew very cool in after years, and finally died out altogether. On whose side the fault lay I will not venture to decide, but in some of the letters to his parents Chopin complains bitterly of Liszt.

Having given up performing in public Chopin occupied himself with giving lessons. His handsome gentlemanly appearance, his great talents and

brilliant fame, and his gift for teaching caused him
to be greatly esteemed and sought after, particularly
by the aristocracy. In taking pupils he always gave
the preference to his compatriots, and trained many
of his own countrywomen who have more or less
acquired his style and manner. Especially to be
mentioned are, Princess Marcelline Czartoryska *née*
Radziwill, the Countess Pauline Plater, Countess
L. Czosnowska, Countess Delphine Potocka, Princess
Beauvau, Madame Rosengart-Zaleska, Emilie Hof-
mann, Baroness Bronicka, &c. Among his non-
Polish pupils were: Madame Kalergi *née* Countess
Nesselrode, afterwards Madame de Muchanoff,
Mdlles. Emma and Laura Harsford, Mademoiselle
Caroline· Hartmann, Mademoiselle Lina Freppa,
Countess Flahault, Baroness C. de Rothschild,
Miss J. W. Sterling, Mademoiselle de Noailles,
Mademoiselle L. Duperré, Mademoiselle R. de Kön-
neritz, Princess Elizabeth Czernicheff, Countess
d'Agoult, Princess C. de Souzzo, Countess d'Appony,
Baroness d'Est, Mdlle. J. de Caraman, Mdlle. C.
Maberly, Countess de Perthuis, Countess de Lobau,
Countess Adele de Fürstenstein, and Mdlle. F.
Müller, to whom Chopin dedicated his Allegro de
Concert op. 46, and who has frequently been spoken
of as his most gifted and favourite lady pupil.

Unlike other great artists, Chopin felt no dislike
to giving lessons, but, on the contrary, took evident
pleasure in this laborious occupation, when he met
with talented and diligent pupils. He noticed the

slightest fault, but always in the kindest and most encouraging manner, and never displayed anger towards a dull pupil. But later on, when increasing illness had made his nerves extremely irritable, he would fling the music from the desk and make use of very severe expressions. Not pencils merely, but even chairs were broken by Chopin's apparently weak hand; however, these outbursts of temper never lasted long; a tear in the eye of the culprit at once appeased the master's wrath, and his kind heart was anxious to make amends.

He could not endure thumping, and on one occasion jumped up during a lesson, exclaiming, " What was that, a dog barking ? " Owing to the delicacy of his nerves his playing was not so powerful as that of other pianists, Liszt especially. This rendered the first few lessons a real torture to his pupils. He found most fault with a too noisy touch; his own thin slender fingers rested horizontally on the keys, which he seemed to stroke rather than strike. Nevertheless he was quite able to produce vigorous tones. It is a great error to suppose that his playing was invariably soft and tender, although, in after years, when he had not sufficient physical power for performing the energetic passages, it lacked contrast, but in his youth he displayed considerable fire and energy, of which he never made any misuse.

Moscheles, in speaking of his playing at a *soirée* at the Palace of King Louis Philippe in 1839, says, " The audience must, I think, have caught the enthusiasm which Chopin threw into the piece throughout."

He would not take a pupil who had not some amount of technical skill, yet he made them all alike begin with Clementi's ": Gradus ad Parnassum." We see from this that his chief object was the cultivation of the touch. The pre-eminence attached to technical superiority by pianists of the present day obliges them to devote their whole time to acquiring mechanical dexterity and enormous force. Thus they frequently lose their softness and lightness of touch, and neglect the finer *nuances* and the artistic finish of the phrasing.

The second requirement that Chopin made of a new pupil was perfect independence of the fingers; he, therefore, insisted on the practising of exercises, and more especially the major and minor scales from *piano* up to *fortissimo*, and with the *staccato* as well as the *legato* touch, also with a change of accent, sometimes marking the second, sometimes the third or fourth note. By this means he obtained the perfect independence of the fingers, and an agreeable equality and delicacy of touch. Chopin thought of embodying in a theoretical work the results of his long years of study, experience, and observation of pianoforte playing; but he had only written a few pages when he fell ill. Unfortunately, he destroyed the manuscript shortly before his death.

Every poetical composition is a revelation of the beautiful which the player ought to recognise, and as far as possible interpret in the spirit of the composer. To the many requests made to him for advice Chopin invariably replied, " Play as you feel and you will play well." One day, when one of his pupils was playing in a stiff, feelingless, mechanical manner, he impatiently exclaimed, " Mettez y donc toute votre âme."

His friends relate that he used to lament greatly over one pupil, who studied with indefatigable diligence and perseverance, and possessed all the qualities for becoming an artist of the first rank except the most essential of all—feeling.

Yet how much mischief may arise from following this true and simple maxim, " Play as you feel." How many celebrated pianists exaggerate or misunderstand the meaning of Chopin's works! His principle is only a sure and infallible guide when the player has the capacity of perceiving the intentions of the composer. This, unfortunately, is a rare gift, and its absence in the rendering of Chopin's compositions is doubly painful. He felt this himself, and when one of his French pupils was being overwhelmed with praise for his performance of one of his master's works, Chopin said, quickly, that he had played the piece very well, but had quite missed the Polish element and the Polish enthusiasm. Nor did he confine this criticism to the interpretation of distinctively Polish works, such as mazurkas and polonaises, but applied it also to his concertos, nocturnes, ballads, and studies.

La Mara* was not wrong in saying that a correct performance of Chopin's works was rarely to be had. No one, be he ever so great a pianist, who cannot sympathise with the misfortunes which have been and are still the lot of the Pole, no one who does not understand the melancholy characteristic of the whole nation, can interpret Chopin with faithfulness.

One evening, in 1833 or 1834, there were assembled at the house of the Castellan Count Plater three great artists : Liszt, Hiller, and Chopin.  A lively discussion arose on national music, Chopin maintaining, that no one who had not been in Poland and inhaled the perfume of its meadows could have any true sympathy with its folk-songs.  As a test of this it was proposed to play the well-known Mazurka, " Poland is not lost yet."  Liszt played first, then Hiller, each giving a different interpretation.  Several pianists followed; last of all came Chopin, whom both Liszt and Hiller were obliged to admit far surpassed them in comprehending the spirit of the Mazurka.

There is, undoubtedly, a growing interest among the public in Chopin's original compositions, but the number of his interpreters who really understand him is still very small.  In some we find a certain affectation and coquetry, in others only the poetic frenzy (schwärmerei) which is infused into most of

---

* " Musikalische Studienköpfe."  Leipzig.

his works, while others again seek expression by
means of violent contrasts.  These apparent diversi-
ties are rarely combined in one individual, but it is
only in their union that we find the true Chopin
stamp of genius.

As the best means for acquiring a natural style
our master recommended the frequent hearing of
Italian singers, among whom there were at that
time many celebrities in Paris.  He always ap-
plauded their broad, simple style and the easy
manner in which they used and consequently preserved their voices, as worthy the imitation of all
pianists, especially of those who hoped to attain
perfection.  He advised his pupils not to break up
the musical thoughts, but to let them pour out in a
broad stream ; he liked to hear in a player what in a
singer is understood by *portamento*.  He hated any
exaggeration of accent which, in his opinion, destroyed all the poetry of playing and made it appear
pedantic.

Chopin's soft velvety fingers could evoke the most
exquisite effects.  No other pianist of the day
possessed his executive skill and refined taste, or
equalled him in those passing embellishments which
he interwove into his playing, and which resembled
filagree work or the most delicate Brabant lace.  He
was very fond of playing to himself or some favourite
pupil the works of Sebastian Bach, which he had
studied with the utmost accuracy and completely

mastered.* The *tempo rubato* was a special characteristic of Chopin's playing. He would keep the
bass quiet and steady, while the right hand moved
in free *tempo,* sometimes with the left hand, and
sometimes quite independently, as, for example,
when it plays quaver, trills, or those magic, rhythmical runs and *fioritures* peculiar to Chopin. " The
left hand," he used to say, " should be like a band-
master, and never for a moment become unsteady or
falter."

By this means his playing was free from the
trammels of measure and acquired its peculiar charm.
The outlines, like those in a good painting of a
winter landscape, shade off into a transparent mist.
He used the *tempo rubato* with great effect, not only
in his nocturnes but also in many of his mazurkas.
Those who have entered into the spirit of Chopin's
works will easily see when to use the *rubato*. Chopin
rendered the *tremolo* to perfection, making the
melody float like a boat on the bosom of the waters.
Liszt says :—

" Chopin was the first to use the *tempo rubato*, which
gave such an original stamp to his compositions : an
evanescent, interrupted measure, ductile, abrupt, yet
languishing, and flickering like a flame in the breeze.

---

* Lenz once said to Chopin, "Do you study much just
before a concert?" He answered, "It is a dreadful time
for me ; I do not like public life, but it is a part of my profession. I shut myself up for a fortnight and play Bach. That
is my preparation. I do not practise my own compositions.

T

In his later works he left off marking *tempo rubato* at the commencement of a piece, considering that whoever understood it would of himself discover this law of latitude. Chopin's works require to be played with a certain accent and swing which it is difficult for anyone to acquire who has not had frequent opportunities of hearing him play. He seemed very anxious to impart this style to his pupils, and especially to his compatriots. His Polish pupils, particularly the ladies, acquired this method with all the quick sensitiveness which they possess for poetic feeling; and their innate perception of his thoughts enabled them to follow faithfully all the undulations on his azure sea of sentiment."

While Chopin was strong and healthy, as during the first years of his residence in Paris, he used to play on an Erard piano; but after his friend Camillo Pleyel had made him a present of one of his splendid instruments, remarkable for their metallic ring and very light touch, he would play on no other maker's. If he were engaged for a *soirée* at one of his Polish or French friends, he would often send his own instrument, if there did not happen to be a Pleyel in the house. "Quand je suis mal disposé," said Chopin, "je joue sur un piano d'Erard et j'y trouve facilement un son fait. Mais quand je me sens en verve et assez fort, pour trouver mon propre son à moi, il me faut un piano de Pleyel."

Chopin sacredly cherished art as one of heaven's best gifts, as a gentle comforter in sorrow, and would never put it to any common-place purpose. There

are, unfortunately, plenty of famous artists who
regard their art merely as a means of subsistence.
What Schiller says of men of science is no less true
of artists :—

"Einem ist sie die hohe, die himmlische Göttin, dem Andern
Eine Tüchtige Kuh, die ihn mit Butter versorgt."

Throughout his life art was to Chopin a lofty
goddess. He was frequently asked by wealthy and
aristocratic personages to give instruction to them
or to their relations, but the largest honorarium could
not induce him to teach anyone devoid of talent;
although at that time he had long ceased to receive
anything from his parents, was very particular about
the appointments of his household, fond of giving
presents, and always dispensed a most liberal hospitality. In a pleasant manner—and, indeed, no other
was possible to him—Chopin would refuse on the
score of not increasing the number of his pupils.
Young people of talent he would encourage with the
sincerest kindness, lending them books, music, and
sometimes money even, when he found their means
were limited ; many he taught gratuitously. One of
his most talented pupils was Filtsch,* a young
Hungarian; Chopin thought a great deal of him, and
always delighted in his company. His premature
death made a deep and painful impression on our
master. All who knew Filtsch intimately, and had

---

* Liszt said of him : " If he travels I shall shut up shop."
(Lenz's " Great Pianists of the present day.")

heard his beautiful playing, say that he would have fulfilled the most splendid hopes, and unite in deploring his death as a sad loss to the musical world.

Among Chopin's best pupils we must name: Gutmann, Guntsberg; Telefsen; George Mathias, who is now a professor at the Paris Conservatoire; Charles Mikuli, director of the Musical Union, at Lemberg; Casimir Wernick, who died young, at St. Petersburg, in 1859; and Gustav Schumann, a much esteemed pianist in Berlin, who only went to Paris for a short time to receive instruction from Chopin.

Chopin was not only respected but loved by all his pupils for his warm sympathy and exceedingly fascinating manners. To Polish artists he was especially amiable and kind, and ever ready to serve them in any way; thus, showing that his love for his fatherland was as warm as when a dreamy, gentle boy, his parents' house in Poland was all the world to him. So it came to pass that many artists, who were only spending a short time in Paris, but were anxious to acquire fame and popularity, gave themselves out as Chopin's pupils, although he did not even know their names. When asked if such a one were his pupil, he would answer, " I never taught him, but if it is any benefit to him to be called my pupil, let him enjoy it in peace." Chopin was not only a kind, but also a conscientious teacher. He never gave more than four or, at the utmost, five lessons a day for his health's sake, but he attended regularly to those and never put off his pupils, except when he was very ill, or when friends and acquaintances from Poland came to see him. Carriages were frequently sent for him by those of his pupils living at a distance, but in the last years of his life they were obliged to come to him, and when he became so weak that he could scarcely sit up, he would give lessons lying on a *chaise longue* before a pianette, with the pupil seated at another instrument. If a passage were played wrongly or not according to his taste, he would raise himself up and play it, and then lie down again.

His noble character and truly artistic nature appeared on all occasions; the following episode is a proof of his excellent disposition. Julius Schulhoff came to Paris when a young man, and completely unknown. One day he heard that Chopin, who was at that time in very bad health and difficult of access, was going to Mercier's* piano manufactory to see a newly invented *transpositeur*. This was in 1844. Schulhoff availed himself of this opportunity for making the master's acquaintance, and was among the little band awaiting the arrival of Chopin, who came accompanied by an old friend, a Russian bandmaster. Seizing a favourable moment, Schulhoff asked a lady present to introduce him. To her request that he should play something to Chopin, the great artist, who was frequently tormented by

---

* This establishment is not in existence now.

the visitations of *dilettanti*, reluctantly acceded by a slight nod. Schulhoff sat down to the piano, while Chopin, with his back to him, leant against it. But after the first few chords he turned his head to Schulhoff, who was playing his new "Allegro brillant en forme de Sonate," which he afterwards dedicated to Chopin as op. 1.* Chopin drew nearer and nearer, listening with growing interest to the refined, poetical playing of the young Bohemian; his pale face lighted up, and by look and gesture he testified his warm approval. When Schulhoff had finished, Chopin held out his hand, saying, "Vous êtes un vrai artiste—un collègue." A few days afterwards Schulhoff paid him a visit, and begged him to accept the dedication of the "Allegro;" the master thanked him in his most winning manner, and some ladies present heard him say, "Je suis très flatté de l'honneur que vous me faites."

---

* Published by S. Richault, in Paris, and by Stern & Co., Berlin.

## CHAPTER XVII.

*DOMESTIC SORROWS. TWO LETTERS OF GEORGE
SAND. BREACH WITH GEORGE SAND. JOURNEY
TO ENGLAND. RETURN TO PARIS. CHOPIN'S
ILLNESS AND DEATH..*

THE fears of the Physicians began to be realized.
Chopin's manner of life in Paris was quite
contrary to their advice, and the saddest results
ensued. In 1840 decided symptoms of an affection
of the lungs appeared. The sufferer was much
troubled by sleeplessness, and during those restless
nights his active and versatile imagination conjured
up the gloomiest fancies. The gravity of the situation was now unmistakeable. His annual visit to
Nohant always gave him some relief; there he could
live in perfect freedom, and work or rest as he felt
inclined. But the winter unfortunately increased
his sufferings, and the sharp cold winds destroyed all
the good effected by the mild air of Nohant.

On May 3rd, 1844, Frederic received a heavy
shock in the death of his dearly beloved father. The
sad intelligence quite prostrated him; and he was

agonized by the thought that he had not been able to soothe his parent's last moments, and receive his blessing and farewell. Frederic felt that he ought to write to comfort his mother and sisters, and mingle his tears with theirs, if only by letter; but, as often as he resolved to do so, his strength failed him. · At length George Sand, who was at that time still faithful to Chopin, undertook the sad duty, and wrote expressing her sympathy with the mother of the man whom once she had so passionately loved, and for whom she still cherished friendship and respect. The following is an exact transcription of her letter:

*Paris, le 29 Mai,* 1844.

MADAME !

Je ne crois pas pouvoir offrir d'autre consolation à l'excellente mère de mon cher Frédéric, que l'assurance du courage et de la résignation de cet admirable enfant. Vous savez si sa douleur est profonde et si son âme est accablée; mais grâce à Dieu, il n'est pas malade, et nous partons dans quelques heures pour la compagne, où il se reposera enfin d'une si terrible crise.

Il ne pense qu'à vous, à ses soeurs, à tous les siens, qu'il chérit si ardemment, et dont l'affliction l'inquiète et le préoccupe autant que la sienne propre.

Du moins, ne soyez pas de votre côté inquiète de sa situation extérieure. Je ne peux pas lui ôter cette peine si profonde, si légitime et si durable ; mais je puis du moins soigner sa santé et l'entourer d'autant d'affection et de précautions que vous le feriez vous même. ·

C'est un devoir bien doux que je me suis imposé avec bonheur et auquel je ne manquerai jamais.

Je vous le promets, Madame, et j'espère que vous avez confiance en mon dévouement pour lui. Je ne vous dis pas que votre malheur m'a frappée autant que si j'avais connu l'homme admirable que vous pleurez. Ma sympathie, quelque vraie qu'elle soit, ne peut adoucir ce coup terrible, mais en vous disant que je consacrerai mes jours à son fils, et que je le regarde comme le mien propre, je sais que je puis vous donner de ce côté-là quelque tranquillité d'esprit. C'est pourquoi j'ai pris la liberté de vous écrire pour vous dire que je vous suis profondément dévouée, comme à la mère adorée de mon plus cher ami.

GEORGE SAND.

Among Chopin's friends and admirers was Alexander Thies,* of Warsaw. He had often seen Frederic in Paris, and through him had become acquainted with George Sand, whom as a writer he greatly admired. He wrote from Warsaw a kind letter of inquiry about Chopin and Mickiewicz, and in conclusion wished good health, prosperity, and fame to George Sand. I mention these three words particularly that the following reply may be intelligible.

---

* Alexander Thies, born in Warsaw, 1804, died in Paris, 1846, a Polish pianist and State functionary. He published, in addition to many scientific articles in home and foreign journals, "Dernier Mot sur le pouvoir social" (Paris, 1836), "Code civil de l'empire de Russie" (Paris, 1841), "Précis des notions historiques sur la formation du corps des lois russes" (Petersbourg, 1843.)

*Paris, le 25 Mars, 1845.*

Monsieur !

Nous sommes bien coupables envers vous, moi
surtout; car lui *(Chopin),* écrit si peu et il a tant
d'excuses dans son état continuel de fatigue et de
souffrance, que vous devez lui pardonner. J'espérais
toujours l'amener à vous écrire, mais je n'ai eu que
des résolutions et des promesses, et je prends le parti
de commencer, sauf à ne pas obtenir, entre sa toux et
ses leçons, un instant de repos et de calme.

C'est vous dire que sa santé est toujours aussi
chancelante. Depuis les grands froids qu'il a fait ici,
il a été surtout accablé; j'en suis presque toujours
malade aussi, et aujourd'hui je vous écris avec un reste
de fièvre. Mais vous ? Vous souffrez plus que nous,
et vous en parlez à peine. Vous êtes un stoïque de
chrétien, et il y a bien d'assez belles et grandes choses
dans votre doctrine, pour que je vous passe la forme,
sur ce point. Vous ne me convertirez pas. Mais que
vous importe ? Vous n'êtes pas, je l'espère, de ces
catholiques farouches, qui damnent sans retour les
dissidents. D'ailleurs, l'orthodoxie de ces principes
d'intolérance est tres-controversée, et votre grand coeur
peut prendre là-dessus le parti qui lui convient ; moi,
j'ai l'espoir d'être sauvée tout comme une autre, bien
que j'ai fait le mal plus d'une fois tout comme une
autre. Mais il y a plus de miséricorde là-haut qu'il n'y
a de crimes ici-bas. Autrement, ce ne serait pas la
justice divine, ce serait la justice humaine, la peine
du faible. Blasphème inique et que je repousse avec
horreur.

Je ne vóus dirai rien de *Mickiewicz*, il n'a pas fait
son cours cette année, et je ne l'ai pas vu*. Je n'ai
même pas lu son livre. Je le regarde aussi comme un
noble malade, mais sans le croire sur le chemin de la
vérité, je le crois aussi bien que vous et moi sur la route
du salut; s'il est dans son erreur convaincu, humble et
aimant Dieu, Dieu ne l'abandonnera pas, Dieu ne boude
pas, er je ne puis croire qu'une telle âme ne soulève pas
quelque coin du voile étrange dont il s'enveloppait
l'année dernière.

Je vous remercie de vos souhaits affectueux, santé
bien-être et gloire; tout cela est chimère. Nous sommes
ici-bas pour souffrir et travailler; la santé est une béné-
diction du ciel, en tant qu'elle nous rend utiles à ceux
qui ne l'ont pas; le bien-être est impossible à quiconque
veut assister ses frères, car dans ce cas-là, plus il peut
recevoir, plus il doit donner. La gloire est une niaiserie
pour amuser les enfants. Une âme sérieuse ne peut y
voir autre chose que le résultat douloureux de l'ignorance des hommes, prompts à s'engouer de peu de chose.
La santé serait donc le seul bien désirable dans vos trois
souhaits. Mais je ne l'ai pas cette année et je ne
murmure pas, puisque vous, qui le méritez mieux que
moi, vous ne l'avez pas retrouvée.

---

* From December, 1840, till March, 1844, Mickiewicz
lectured at the Collége de France, on Slavic literature. His
wide-spread fame and his ability as a lecturer attracted
crowded audiences. But he sank into a morbid mysticism,
and talked of a visionary milennium instead of literature, and
was, on that account, suspended by the authorities. His
lectures are published under the title of "Les slaves. Cours
professé au Collége de France." (Paris, 1849.)

Espérez-vous maintenant en cette cure que vous avez
entreprise avec tant de courage ?   Ecrivez-moi donc que
vous êtes mieux ; cela nous consolerait de n'être pas
bien.   Eh quand nous revenez-vous ?   Nous n'irons pas
de bonne heure à la campagne, si le printemps est aussi
laid que l'hiver.   J'espère donc que nous vous reverrons
ici, et si vous tardez, nous voulons vous voir à Nohant.
Vous devez nous dédommager d'y être restés si peu
l'autre fois.   Mes enfants vous remercient de votre bon
souvenir et font aussi des voeux pour vous.

A vous de coeur, toujours et bien sincèrement, vous
le savez.

GEORGE SAND.

The letters of George Sand show that Chopin's
condition was already regarded as hopeless.   Soon
after the death of his father, the poor invalid, who
so much needed comforting and cheering, had to
bear another grief in the loss of his dearest friend
in Paris, Johann Matuszynski.   As his physical
sufferings increased, he grew melancholy and was
haunted by the most dismal imaginations.   George
Sand speaks of this in writing to a friend who knew
him well :

"The Catholic faith, by teaching the doctrine of a
purgatorial fire, represents death in a terrible light.
Far from picturing the soul of a beloved one in a
better world, Chopin often had dreadful visions, and
I was obliged to spend the night near his sleeping
apartment, to dispel the spectres of his dreaming and
waking hours.   He dwells a great deal on the super-

stitions of Polish tradition.   The spirits harass and
entangle him in their magic circle, and instead of
seeing his father and friend smiling at him from the
abodes of the glorified, as the Lutheran doctrine teaches,
he imagines that their lifeless forms are at his bed-side,
or that he is tearing himself from their cold embrace."

Month by month the disease made rapid strides,
and his strength perceptibly diminished.   The cough
grew more obstinate, and very often he was so weak
and suffered so from want of breath, that when he
went to see his friends he was obliged to be carried
upstairs.

The following are the compositions written between 1843 and 1847 : Polonaise, op. 53 ; Berceuse,
op. 57 ; Sonata in B minor, op. 58 ; Mazurkas, op.
59 and 63 ; Barcarole, op. 60 ; Polonaise-Fantasia,
op. 61, and Sonata in G minor for piano and violin-
cello, op. 65.   These pieces are throughout beautiful,
and poetical, but the melancholy and peculiar agitation displayed, especially in the two last, reveal
the morbid mind of the composer.   The musical
thoughts have not the pleasing clearness of his earlier
works and not infrequently border on eccentricity.
But how full of sorrow and suffering had these years
been to the delicately wrought spirit of the artist
with its natural inclination to melancholy.

Chopin who, in spite of his self-absorption, noticed
everything that went on around him—his innate
sensitiveness of feeling supplying the place of observation—could no longer conceal from himself, that

the woman who had attracted him by the intensity
of her love, and won the devotion of his deeply
poetical nature, that she, whose steadfastness had
seemed firm as a rock, was daily wavering in her
affection.  His pride whispered, "leave her, she
regards you as a burden;" but the moral feeling
fostered by his education, and his parents' noble
example of wedded faithfulness and constancy,
exorted him to stay.

There were times during his youth when Chopin
felt some scruples about his illegitimate connection
with Aurora Dudevant-Sand, when he sincerely
wished that he could lead her to the altar, and
cursed the fate which hindered him.  Afterwards
he consoled himself with the thought that the firm-
ness of the bond on both sides made it sacred, and
unquestionably nothing on earth would have moved
him to separate from her.

George Sand thought otherwise.  This fanciful
woman, with her keen susceptibilities for the beautiful, had loved the young, interesting, and celebrated
composer; but the dejected invalid was an incum-
brance.  Her change of feeling was first manifested
by occasional sullen looks and by the increasing
shortness of her visits to the sick room.  Chopin
felt much pained, but was silent, for according to his
ideas it would have been dishonourable on his part
to cause a breach.  His strength of will was im-
paired by broken health, and he submitted patiently
to innumerable little mortifications which, however,

wounded him deeply; his moral sense told him that he ought to atone for the wrong he had done in taking this woman unlawfully to himself.

He was grieved at the complaints she often made in his presence of the fatigue of nursing him; he begged her to leave him alone and go out into the open air; he entreated her not to give up her amusements for his sake, but to go to the theatre and give parties, &c.; he should be quiet and contented if he knew that she were happy. At last, before the sick man had dreamed of a separation, an heroic expedient, as Count |Stanisla Tarnowski says, was resorted to. George Sand had written a romance, entitled, "Lucrezia Floriani," of which the following is a brief summary.

"Prince Charles, a man of a noble and sympathetic character, but sickly, nervous, jealous, proud, and full of aristocratic notions, falls passionately in love with Lucrezia, a woman no longer young, who has given up love and the world, and lives only for her children and to do good. She is a famous artist, who does not pretend to be better than she is, but who is better than she is said to be. This consuming love causes Prince Charles a severe illness which endangers his life. Lucrezia saves him and loves him; but, foreseeing that this love would be a misery to her, conceals it. Prince Charles's feelings, however, growing more and more passionate and again threatening his safety, the object of his adoration gives herself up to him."

It is strange how women of a certain age like to

hide their feelings under the cloak of sacrifice and
motherly care. *They* are not in love, but the weak,
sick, nervous being needs support and tenderness.
Thus is produced that painful and disagreeable
counterfeit of motherly affection which we so often
meet with, as in "Lucrezia Floriani."

"Whence," asks the writer of the romance, "arises
this unnatural specious feeling? Perhaps if a heroine
loves at that age, when, as Hamlet says, 'the hey-
day in the blood is tame,' she feels degraded in her
own eyes and in those of the world, and to regain
her position, and gloss over her real feelings and
actions, she makes a pretext of sacrifice and tender
care." In this way the famous Madame de Warrens
interpreted her sacrifice, of which J. J. Rousseau says
so much in his "Confessions;" and thus Lucrezia
explained her love for Charles.

For two months she was unspeakably happy; then
everything changed. Charles grows jealous, un-
reasonable, and capricious; he cannot bear the
sight of Lucrezia's old friends. There are constant
outbursts of anger and nervous excitement, or fits of
madness and desperation. Wearied and harassed,
Lucrezia's health and strength give way; but of
this she makes a secret and never complains because
she has vowed to make any sacrifice for Charles.
She knows that she will die—for Charles will make
a martyr of her—and that her children will be
orphans, yet she goes on suffering in silence because
she has pledged herself to be faithful to him. After

a few years of a life of such constant torture, and of
alienation from her friends on account of the jealousy
of Charles, she ceases to love him and submits
resignedly to her fate. At length, exhausted by pro-
tracted self sacrifice, Lucrezia dies.

It was at that time generally thought that Prince
Charles was a portrait of Chopin, although the
exaggeration with which the character was drawn
made it a caricature. The love story in the romance
certainly bore a strong resemblance to the connection
between himself and George Sand, which, with all
its happiness, was, as none better than he knew,
a very painful one. Both Frederic and the world
were well aware that the real Lucrezia was not
a victim to her devotedness, and that the Charles
of the novel could be none other than Chopin. It is
said that, by a refinement of cruelty, the proofs were
sent to him for correction; it is a matter of fact,
however, that George Sand's children said to him,
" Monsieur Chopin, do you know that Prince Charles
is meant for you ? "

Everyone acquainted with the circumstances
blamed the authoress. She excused herself,* saying
that she had been misunderstood, and that the
intention imputed to her had no existence.

" But," said she by way of justification, " Charles is
not an artist or a genius ; he is only a dreamer. His
character scarcely rises above the common-place ; it

---

* " Histoire de ma vie." Vol. XIII.

never appears amiable, and has, indeed, so little in
common with that of the great composer, that Chopin,
although he every day reads the manuscript off my
writing table and is very suspicious about other things,
never imagined that any reference was intended to himself. Afterwards, indeed, the malicious whisperings of
some of his friends, who were enemies to me, made him
fancy, that in Prince Charles I was describing him, and
in the martyr Lucrezia, myself; and that this romance
depicted the relations between us. His memory was at
that time very weak, and when a garbled version of the
story was presented to him, he had quite forgotten the
real description of the character and circumstances of
Prince Charles. Why did he not read my novel again?"

Madame Sand much regretted that Matuszynski
was not living when a breach between herself and
Chopin had become inevitable. " His friendship for
Chopin and the influence he had over him would,"
said the authoress, " have rendered innocuous the
whisperings of intriguers, and if a separation had
taken place at all, his mediation would have made
it less violent and painful."

The sick and enfeebled artist suffered, however,
most keenly from the mortification which he received
from this book. " If," he reflected, " I now desert
the woman whom I formerly esteemed and loved,
I make the romance a reality, and expose her to the
blame, nay, even the scorn of the strictly virtuous."
He nobly struggled on, retreating more and more
into himself, till at last he could bear it no longer.

In the beginning of 1847, during a violent scene, of which her daughter was the innocent cause, George Sand brought about a complete rupture. To her unjust reproaches he only replied, " I shall leave your house immediately, and I only desire that my existence may be blotted out from your memory." To these words George Sand offered no objection, for they were just what she desired, and the same day the artist quitted her for ever.

Agitation and grief again laid him on a sick bed, and his friends were long and seriously afraid that he would only exchange it for his coffin. Gutmann, his favourite pupil, and one of his best friends, nursed him with the most devoted care ; and the deep gratitude of the sufferer was shown by the questions which he continually asked of the friends and acquaintances who came to see him. "How is Gutmann? Is he not very tired? Will it not be too much for him if he sits up with me any longer ? I am sorry to give him so much trouble, but there is no one else I like so well to have about me as him." These were almost the only words he spoke, for his visitors would not let him talk, and did all they could to amuse him and divert his mind.

Through the efforts of the physicians and the indefatigable attentions of Gutmann, Chopin at length somewhat recovered. But the first time he appeared again among his friends he was so much altered that they hardly knew him. The following summer he was apparently much better, and able to

compose; but he would not leave Paris, as was his
constant habit at that time of year, and was thus
deprived of the fresh country air which had always
been so beneficial to him.

During the winter of 1847-1848 Chopin was in a
very precarious state of health.   Political disturbances and other causes made his residence in Paris
increasingly unpleasant, and he resolved on visiting
England, where he had many very kind friends, who
had repeatedly invited him to come whenever he had
time.   But before leaving the queen of Continental
cities he wished to give a farewell public concert.*
It took place on February 16th, 1848, at the Pleyel
Hall, and Chopin could not have desired a more
select and distinguished audience, or a more enthusiastic reception.†   Many of the most exalted

---

* It cannot be said that Chopin obtruded himself on the
public notice; for, from 1834 to 1848, he only gave one public
concert (Feb. 21st, 1842) with the assistance of Viardot-Garcia
and Franchomme, when Chopin performed the following compositions : Ballade (A flat major); three mazurkas (A flat, B,
A minor); three studies (A flat, F minor, C minor); prelude
(D flat) ; impromptu (G flat) ; nocturne (D flat.)   As this
concert naturally made a much better impression than the
first given in the Italian theatre, on account of Chopin's
poetical and expressive playing, he held *séances* in the Pleyel
Hall nearly every year, when he always played alone, and his
admirers and friends paid twenty francs for their tickets.

† Chopin's last concert began with one of Mozart's trios, in
which Alard and Franchomme took part.   Then Chopin played
his new 'cello-sonata in G minor (op. 65), and some smaller
pieces—studies, preludes, mazurkas, and waltzes.

personages and the first artists in Paris were present, and throughout the performance all were anxious to testify their respect and admiration for the talented composer, the rare *virtuoso* and the loveable man. Frederic was deeply affected; this, the last of his Parisian triumphs, was a balsam for many of the wounds of fate which, although gradually healing, were still sometimes very painful.

Chopin was greatly shocked by the political events of February 23rd, which overthrew a dynasty, and sent a monarch and his family into exile. From Louis Philippe and his kindred he had experienced nothing but affability and kindness, and Frederic deplored the fate of the Orleanists. At the same time, however, this revolution awakened fresh hopes for his unfortunate country, which he loved as passionately and faithfully as when, a youth in Warsaw, he set to music patriotic songs which it was unsafe to publish. But when he saw that the storm which swept over Europe brought neither freedom nor independence to Poland, he suppressed his longings, and in talking of politics rarely gave vent to the feelings of his over-charged heart.

There was now nothing to prevent his journey to England. His friends, much as they liked his company, did not dissuade him from his purpose, and hoped that he would soon feel at home in London. At the latter end of March, just a month before his departure, he was invited to a *soirée* by a lady, at whose hospitable house he had, in former days, been a frequent guest. He hesitated before deciding to go, for during the last four years he had not been often seen in the Parisian *salons;* then, as if moved by an inward premonition, he accepted the invitation.

A lively conversation about Chopin had been going on at Madame H.'s before he arrived. A musical connoisseur was describing his meeting with the famous artist at Nohant, and his wonderful playing on the beautiful summer moonlight night. A lady observed : " Chopin's spirit pervades the best of Sand's romances. Like all highly imaginative writers, she often lost patience over her work, because before she had carried out one plan her mind was advancing to something fresh. To keep herself to her desk and to enable her to write with more care, she would ask her lover to improvise on the piano, and thus, inspired by his playing, she produced her best novels."

A deep, half audible, sigh escaped from a lady, who, unobserved by the speaker, had stepped softly into the *salon* from the adjoining room. A flush overspread her pale face, tears stood in her deep mysterious eyes ; what could have moved her so profoundly ?

Several gentlemen then entered the room, and the lady retreated behind a mass of ivy which formed a convenient screen. She sat there for about an hour, unnoticed except by the hostess, who understood her behaviour. When the company had become more numerous the lady rose, and, walking up to Chopin, with the swinging step peculiar to her, held out her hand. "Frederic," she murmured, in a voice audible only to him, and standing before him he saw, for the first time, after a long and painful separation, George Sand, repentant, and evidently anxious for reconciliation. His delicate, emaciated, yet still beautiful face, grew deadly pale; for a moment his soft eyes met hers with an inquiring look, and then he turned away and left the room in silence.

Towards the end of April he bade adieu to his friends and set off for London. In England Chopin's works already enjoyed a well-deserved esteem and popularity; he was, therefore, everywhere received with unusual marks of respect and with that hearty sympathy which is the best reward of the poet and artist. The hospitality and kindness of his old friends, and the courtesy of his new acquaintances, were very grateful to Frederic's sensitive and affectionate nature. He again appeared in society, and hoped that, while pursuing his beloved art amid fresh surroundings, he might forget the woman for whom, notwithstanding all the wrong she had done him, he sometimes ardently longed. He could not, despite all his efforts, erase from his memory the period of almost supernal happiness once created for him by her dazzling intellect, exhaustless fancy, and ardent love, although his reason constantly told him that she was not worthy of a sigh.

After he had been presented to the Queen by the

Duchess of Sutherland, and had played at Court, he daily received invitations from the first families, and became, finally, a noted favourite. The late evening parties, the want of sleep, and the wear and tear of *salon* life, were very injurious to his weak constitution, and quite opposed to the doctors' orders. For the sake of quiet he accepted an invitation to Scotland, but, as might have been expected, the climate was too severe for him. The prevalent mists, so trying to nervous temperaments, affected his spirits, and induced that melancholy which had often troubled him in early years, and become infused into his earnest and widly romantic compositions. He writes from Scotland to his friend Grzymala :—

" I have played at a concert in Glasgow before all the *haute volée*. To-day I feel very much depressed. Oh, this fog! Although the window at which I am writing commands the same beautiful prospect with which, as you will remember, Robert Bruce was so delighted — Stirling Castle, mountains, lakes, a charming park, in a word the most splendid view in Scotland—I can see nothing except when the sun breaks momentarily through the mist. If it would but do this a little oftener! I shall soon forget Polish, and speak French like an Englishman, and English like a Scotchman.

" If I do not write you a Jeremiade it is not because I mistrust your sympathy, but because you only know everything ; and if I once begin I shall go on complaining for ever, and always in the same strain. But, no, I am wrong in saying it is always the same, for I grow worse every day. I feel weaker and weaker and cannot compose, not for want of inclination, but from physical causes, and besides I am in a different place every week. But what *am* I to do? I must at least lay by something for the winter."

Despite the kindness and the hospitable welcome which he received from two Scotch ladies, sisters, one of whom, Miss J. W. Stirling, had been, his pupil, he did not enjoy his visit, and sometimes longed for wings that he might fly back to France. I quote again from his letter to Grzymala :—

" I am quite incapable of doing anything all the morning, and when I am dressed I feel so exhausted that I am obliged to rest. After dinner I have to sit two hours with the gentlemen, listen to their conversation, and look on while they drink. I feel ready to die with weariness, and think of other things all the time till I go into the drawing-room, when I have to use all my efforts to rouse myself, for everybody is curious to hear me play. After this, my good Daniel carries me upstairs, undresses and puts me to bed; he leaves the light burning, and I am once more at leisure to sigh and dream, and look forward to passing another day in the same manner. If I ever arrange to do anything I am sure to be carried off in another direction, for my Scotch friends—although with the best intentions in the world—give me no rest. They want to introduce me to all their relations; they will kill me with their kindness, but for mere politeness' sake I must put up with it all."

Witty men never quite lose their sense of humour, and a gleam of cheerfulness, a spark of his former brilliant *esprit*, would now and then shine forth amid his melancholy. He describes going to the opera in London when Jenny Lind made her *début*, and the Queen appeared in public for the first time after a long retirement. He says, "I was very much impressed, especially by old Wellington, who, as a valiant protector of monarchy, sat in front of his sovereign, like a faithful watch-dog guarding his lord's castle. I have made the acquaintance of Jenny Lind; she is from Sweden, and is quite an original."

His *ennui*, however, increased. He wrote to Grzymala :—

"I am going to Manchester where there is to be a grand concert, and I am to play twice without orchestral accompaniment. Alboni is also to perform, but I take no interest in this or anything else. I shall just sit down and play, and what I shall do afterwards I do not yet know. If I were only sure of not being ill if I spent the winter here."

In another letter he complains that he is feeling ill, but has to play at a concert, and he commissions his friend in Paris to look out for a suitable residence. He adds, "why I should trouble you with all this I do not know, for I really do not care about anything. But I must think about myself, so I ask you to help me in doing so." Then comes a

reference to the unhappy love which he cannot forget :
" I never yet cursed anyone, but I am now so overwhelmed by the weariness of life, that I am ready to
curse Lucrezia.  But there is pain in this too, which
is all the worse as one grows older in wickedness
every day."  He finishes by saying, " It is no good
their troubling about me at home.  I cannot be
more wretched than I am, and there is no chance of
my being less so.  In general I feel nothing and await
my end with patience."  And indeed the end was not
far off.  In his last letter from England he writes :—
  " On Thursday I am to leave terrible London.  In
addition to my other ills I have got neuralgia.  Tell
Pleyel to send me in a piano on Thursday evening,
and have it covered ; buy a bunch of violets to make
the room smell sweet.*  I should like when I return
to find some books of poetry in my bedroom to which
I shall, probably, be confined for some time.  So on
Friday evening I hope to be in Paris ; a day longer
here, and I should go mad or die.  My Scotch lady
friends are good, but very wearisome.  They have
made so much of me that I cannot easily get quit of
them.  Let the house be thoroughly warmed and
well dusted.  Perhaps I may get well again.
  This was, alas ! a false hope.  Chopin left London
in the beginning of 1849, after performing for the
last time at a concert he had got up for the benefit

---

* Chopin always wanted flowers about him, and, if possible,
violets.

of the Polish emigrants, and which was very numerously attended. Soon after his return to Paris he suffered a severe loss in the sudden death of the celebrated Dr. Molin, to whose skill and care Chopin owed the prolongation of his life. From that time he despaired of himself. The place of the beloved and honoured physician, whose very presence had been a comfort, could never be supplied.

Hearing that his dear friend, Titus Woycie-chowski, was going to Ostend for the sea-baths, Frederic felt a strong desire to join him. Relative to this we find two letters—the last he ever wrote. As a Russian subject, it was not then very easy for Woyciechowski to go to Paris. He would have required special permission from the authorities at Warsaw, or at least a letter from the Russian Ambassador in Paris:

*Paris, August 20th,* 1849.
*Square d'Orleans, Rue St. Lazare, No.* 9.

MY DEAREST FRIEND,

Nothing but my present severe illness should prevent me from hastening to you at Ostend; but I hope that by the goodness of God you may be enabled to come to me. The doctors will not allow me to travel. I am in my room drinking Pyrenean water, but your presence would do me more good than all the medicines.

Yours till death,
FREDERIC.

*Paris, September 12th,* 1849.

MY DEAR TITUS,

I have not had time to see about obtaining the permission for you to come here. I cannot go for it myself, as I lie in bed half my time, but have asked a friend, who has a good deal of influence, to see about it for me, and shall hear something definite by Sunday. I wanted to go by rail to the frontier at Valenciennes to meet you; but the doctors forbid my leaving Paris, because a few days ago I was not able to get as far as Ville. d'Avraye, near Versailles, where I have a god-son. For this reason they will not send me to a warmer climate this winter.

You see it is only illness that keeps me; had I been tolerably well I should certainly have gone to Belgium to visit you. Perhaps you may be able to come here. I am not egotistical enough to wish that you should come merely for my sake; for, ill as I am, you would be wearied and disappointed, although I think we might pass some pleasant hours, recalling youthful memories, and I wish the time we do have together to be an entirely happy one.

Ever yours, FREDERIC.

From that day the disease made rapid strides. Chopin did not fear death, but seemed in a manner to long for it. The thought of quitting a life so full of sad remembrances was not altogether unwelcome. His moments of respite from pain became fewer and fewer. He spoke with perfect consciousness and calmness about his death and the disposal of his body. He expressed a wish to be buried in the churchyard of Père Lachaise beside Bellini, with whom between 1832 and 1835 he had been very friendly.

He was so much worse by the beginning of October that he could not sit up. His relatives were informed of his condition, and Chopin's eldest sister, Madame Louise Jedrzejewicz, immediately hastened to him with her husband and daughter. The meeting between brother and sister must be imagined rather than described. In 1844 Louise had nursed her beloved brother through a dangerous illness, and afterwards spent a few weeks with him at Nohant. She felt now directly she saw him that he would only need her tender care a short time. Sometimes, when free from pain, he was still cheerful and hopeful. He even took a new house, No. 12, Place Vendôme, and gave minute directions about furnishing it.

At length the last hour approached. His sister and his faithful pupil, Gutmann, never left him for a moment. The Countess Delphine Potocka, who was at some distance from Paris, set off to return the instant she heard of the hopeless condition of the revered master, that she might receive his farewell. In the room adjoining the apartment where Chopin lay speechless, were some friends anxious to see him before he closed his eyes for ever. It was a Sunday, the fifteenth of October, and the streets

were quieter than usual. His sufferings were intense,
yet he tried to smile at the friends around him ; and
when he saw the Countess Potoka, who was standing
beside his sister weeping bitterly, he asked her softly
to sing something. By a strong effort of self-con-
trol she mastered her emotion, and in a ringing
voice of bell-like purity, sang Stradella's Hymn to
the Virgin, so beautifully and so devoutly that the
dying man—artist and lover of the beautiful to the
very last—whispered with delight, "Oh how beautiful!
My God how beautiful ! Again, again." As if endowed
with supernatural strength the Countess sat down to
the piano and sang a psalm by Marcello. Those
standing at his bedside saw that he was growing
weaker every second and sank noiselessly on their
knees. The solemn stillness was broken only by
Delphine Potocka's wonderful voice, which sounded
like that of an angel summoning the great master to
the realms of the blessed ; all suppressed their sobs
that they might not disturb the enjoyment of his
last moments.

Evening was closing in ; his sister knelt by his
bed-side, weeping. The next morning Chopin felt a
little better. He asked for extreme unction, and
Alexander Jelowicki, a very pious and learned priest,
who was held in high esteem by his countrymen,
was sent for. The dying man confessed to him
twice, and, in the presence of his friends, received
the last sacrament. He then called them all one by
one to his bedside and blessed and commended them

to God. After that he quite lost the power of speech and seemed unconscious. But a few hours later he revived and desired the priest to pray with him. Resting his head on Gutmann's shoulder, Chopin, in a clear voice repeated after the priest every word of the Litany. When the last agony commenced he said, "Who is near me?" Then he asked for some water, and when he had moistened his lips he inclined his head and kissed the hand of Gutmann, who was supporting him. After this last sign of gratitude and affection, he sighed once as if released from a burden, and then closed his eyes for ever. At this moment the bells of Paris struck three o'clock in the morning, of October 17th, 1849. A few minutes afterwards the doors of the chamber were opened and the friends and acquaintances in the next room came to look once more on the beloved face of the dead.

It was well known in musical circles that Chopin dearly loved flowers, and the very same morning such quantities were sent that the body of the dead but undying master as it lay in state was literally covered with them. His face, which had been somewhat changed by long illness, assumed an expression of indescribable serenity and youthful loveliness. M. Chesinger took a cast of his countenance, from which he afterwards copied the marble bust which adorns Chopin's tomb.

The reverent admiration which Chopin had always felt for Mozart led him to request, in his last days, that no music but the German master's sublime Requiem should be performed at his funeral. Up till 1849 women had not been allowed to take part in the musical performance at the Madeleine Church, and special permission had to be obtained from the ecclesiastical authorities. On this account the funeral did not take place till October 30th. The first artists in Paris co-operated. The funeral march from Chopin's B flat minor Sonata, which had been scored by Reber for the occasion, was introduced at the Introit. For the Offertory, Léfébure Wély played on the organ Chopin's Preludes in B minor and E minor.* The solos of the Requiem were rendered by Mesdames Pauline Viardot-Garcia and Castellan, and the famous bass singer, Lablache, who gave a splendid delivery of the "Tuba mirum." Meyerbeer conducted, and the pall-bearers were Prince Alexander Czartoryski, Delacroix, Franchomme and Gutmann.

When the remains were lowered into the grave, Polish earth was scattered on the coffin. It was the same that Chopin had brought from Wola nineteen years before as a memorial of his beloved fatherland. He had always guarded it with pious care, and shortly before his death had requested that if he might not rest in Polish soil his body might at least be covered with his native earth. Chopin's heart,

---

* A facsimile of the original draught of the E minor prelude will be found at the end of this volume.

which had beaten so warmly and suffered so deeply
for his country was, according to his desire, sent to
the land whose sun had shone on his happy youth ;
it is preserved *ad interim* in the church of the Sacred
Cross, at Warsaw.

# CHAPTER XVIII.

## *CHOPIN AS A MAN.*

TO what has been written I have little to add.
Chopin was a model son, an affectionate brother,
and a faithful friend. His personal appearance
was so agreeable and harmonious that the eye
rested on him with pleasure. His dark brown eyes *
were cheerful rather than pensive, his smile was
kindly and perfectly good-natured; he had a
complexion of almost transparent delicacy, and
luxuriant brown hair, as soft as silk; his Roman
nose was slightly aquiline; all his movements
were graceful, and he had the manners of an
aristocrat of the highest rank. Everyone with any
discernment of true gentility and real genius could
not but say, on seeing Chopin, " there is a distinguished man." His voice was musical and rather
subdued. He was not above middle height, naturally
delicate, and in his general contour ressembled his
mother.

---

* It is inexplicable why Liszt should have frequently spoken
of his " blue eyes."

One of his lady friends not inaptly remarked that "his disposition was joyous, but his heart full of dreamy yearning," which shows that by his good spirits he diffused cheerfulness around him. Through his nature there ran a vein of melancholy and enthusiasm (schwärmerei) which was very attractive. He had so much amiability and good-breeding, that his physical sufferings, his nervous excitability, and the violent antipathies which he felt in common with all nervous people never, made any difference to his behaviour in daily life. He rarely spoke about his own feelings lest he should be misunderstood.

At some houses in Paris he was a daily guest, and he always spent the evening with friends. Thus he had the *entrée* of twenty or thirty *salons*, where he met with universal kindness and attention, as everybody was fascinated by him. To have transported Frederic Chopin, the darling of princesses and countesses, from these refined surroundings into a simple common-place circle, would have been nothing short of depriving him of the chief end of his existence.

Unlike most great artists, he had an aversion to appearing in public. To give a concert was to him a disagreeable undertaking, which he never entered on without repugnance. He had sufficient pride to enable him to make a dignified appearance; he knew, but did not over-estimate, his own powers, and recognized with friendly fellow-feeling the artistic merits of others.

Accustomed to comfort and elegance, he liked to be surrounded by *objets de luxe*, to have his apartments richly carpeted, and filled with ornamental furniture, costly consoles, and *etagères* covered with presents. He was passionately fond of flowers, and, as I have before mentioned, always had some in his rooms. His dress was stylish and tasteful, and his linen which came from the best shops in Paris, dazzlingly white. He did not agree with those who say that an artist has a right to neglect his appearance. It is said that when he was going to play in public he would order in coats from different tailors, and, having tried them all on and found something to object to in each, he would at the last moment borrow one of his pupil, (Gutmanns), which was a great deal too large for him.

He used, especially when he first came to live in France, to do all he could to help poor Polish emigrants, either by recommendations or with money and clothes. When Princess' Czartoryska opened a bazaar for their benefit at the Hotel Lambert, Chopin spent more than a thousand francs in elegant trifles, which he gave away. His generosity in this direction knew no bounds, and it is not surprising that he left nothing when he died. As a boy he had begun his artistic career with a concert for the poor, and the last he ever gave was for the Polish emigrants in London. It was this ready sympathy that caused the breach with Charles Lipinski, who came to Paris in 1835, and gave some concerts. Chopin proposed that they should give a concert together for the benefit of the Poles, but Lipinski refused, saying, that he did not wish to compromise himself at St. Petersburg, where he intended to perform next year. Chopin was so indignant at this answer that he broke off the friendship, and never forgave Lipinski for his hard-hearted indifference towards his distressed countrymen.

He was always willing to sacrifice himself for his friends, but to strangers he was cool and reserved. If he found people seeking his acquaintance and sending him invitations for the sake of gaining distinction, he soon put an end to the connection. When a rich man, who had asked him to dinner that he might amuse the guests by his playing, pressed him to perform, Chopin replied, "Ah, sir, I have dined so sparingly." But when he was sure that he should give real pleasure he was never stingy in exercising his talents. The famous author, Louis Blanc, writes in his "Histoire de la Revolution, 1848," (vol. II.)

"When the republican, Gottfried Cavaignac (cousin of the celebrated general) was approaching his end, he expressed a wish to hear music once more. Louis Blanc, who was personally acquainted with Chopin, promised to go and find the artist, and bring him back with him, if the doctor would consent. Chopin, being informed by Louis Blanc of the circumstances, set off at once. He was taken into a room with rather a bad piano and sat down to play. Suddenly a loud sob was heard. Moved and excited, Gottfried felt quickened with new life, and sat up, with his eyes full of tears. Chopin was so much affected that he could not go on. Madame Cavaignac bent anxiously over her son, who, mustering up all his strength, said, in a weak voice, ' Don't be troubled, mother; it is nothing. Oh, what a beautiful art is music! Such music and such playing!'"

Frederic was in general not at all fond of letter-writing, and needed some strong motive to induce him to take up his pen. The only correspondence he kept up was with his relations and his friend Woyciechowski; and after 1838 this somewhat fell off, his connection with the great French authoress and his ill-health being probably the cause. He dared not make known to his family the full particulars of his manner of life, and knowing the strict moral principles of his parents, he preferred to keep secret his *liaison* with George Sand. This gave a certain air of embarassment to his letters, which had formerly been so open and unconstrained, that on reading them one seemed both to see and hear him.

"It was often very comical," says Liszt, to see Chopin receive a written invitation to dinner, which he either wished or was obliged to decline; he would take a long walk and excuse himself in person rather than reply by writing."

He often accompanied the letters to his sisters and his nephews and nieces with playthings or articles of dress, and was as delighted as a child if he could prepare some surprise for them. It was a *fête* day for him when a letter came from Warsaw. He never talked about it, but privately devoted his thoughts to those he loved. He valued so highly any present they sent him that he would not suffer any one to touch it or even to look at it for long.

Brought up from a child in the faith of the Romish Church he did not like to talk or argue about religion, but kept his opinions to himself. He rarely took any prominent part in discussions on politics or literature, although he enjoyed listening to them. He never obtruded his ideas on anyone, but if his beloved art were attacked he was instantly up in arms. In the cause of Romanticism he broke many a lance, and gave abundant proof, particularly during the first years of his residence in Paris, of his thorough devotion to the principles of that school. Its most important representatives at that time were Berlioz and Liszt, the ablest, boldest, and most persevering opponents of the Classic school. In 1832 Chopin, who had grown up amid the clamour of this contest, adopted the views of Berlioz and Liszt, and joined the party who openly discarded the old-fashioned style, from which they held as much aloof as from charlatanism. All through the controversy over the Romantic school, some of the productions of which were real masterpieces, Chopin remained staunch to his opinions. He would not make the slightest concession to those who did not follow art for its own sake, but only used it as a means of obtaining money, fame, or honour. Much as he enjoyed the society of fellow artists, he renounced it unhesitatingly if convinced that they were going too far in their resistance to all innovation, and were endeavouring to restrict his own creative efforts. To him art was sacred, and he would never praise a composition or an interpretation which he did not think really worthy of being commended.

Chopin needed no recourse to artificial means to secure the triumph and popularity of his works. To his most intimate friends he would sometimes say, "I believe that my works will stand on their intrinsic merits; whether these be recognized now or in the future is immaterial." A thorough training in youth, a habit of reflection, and his great reverence for the beauties of the classics, effectually preserved him from blindness and error. The extraordinary care and conscientiousness with which he finished his works protected him from the attacks of those superficial or hostile critics who sought eagerly for the smallest mistake. Early accustomed to the sternest self-examination, he threw into his waste-paper basket many compositions which others would perhaps have proudly handed to their printer. He never undertook a work unsuited to his capacities or began anything which he was not sure he could successfully carry out.

Educated by German masters and on German principles, Chopin had a decided preference for the music of that country. Handel, Gluck, Bach, Haydn, and Mozart were his ideals of perfection;

and although he felt the spell of Beethoven's genius,
he had less sympathy with its gigantic conceptions
than with the fascinating charm and lovely melodies
of Mozart's compositions. There seemed to him in
Beethoven's works a want of delicate finish, the proportions were too colossal, and the storms of passion
too violent. About the year 1835, Schubert began
to be known in Paris, principally by his songs. Like
all impartial musicians, Chopin was charmed by
their wealth of melody; but he regretted that in his
larger works, the exuberance of the composer's fancy
frequently led him to overstep the limits of form, and
thus impair the effect.

When Chopin first began to attract the attention
of the musical world in Paris, there were odd stories
current about his parentage. Some thought he was
a German; others, on account of his name, a Frenchman. He always protested energetically against these
suppositions, declaring, with the pride of a good
patriot, that he was a Pole. His nationality and
his love for his country were shown both in word
and deed, appearing not only in his generosity, and
his voluntarily sharing the exile of his unfortunate
countrymen, but also in his choice of friends and his
preference for Polish pupils. However, he was not at
all addicted to boasting of his patriotism. Although
of French descent on his father's side and perfectly
familiar with the language, his accent still betrayed
the nationality of his mother.

Just as he drew musical inspiration from the

Polish folk-songs, so he loved to imitate the simple
speech of the peasants, which he could render to
perfection in its crispness and terseness, if he were
in good spirits. When, for example, in a circle of
intimate friends his playing had created a melancholy
impression, he could at once disperse it by a counterfeit of the peasant dialect, especially that of the
Mazovians and Cracovians. If a discussion arose as
to the comparative merits of the different modern
languages, he would always extol his mother tongue
to the skies, and could never say enough in praise of
its beauty, wealth, sweetness, aptness of expression,
and masculine power.

In common with many imaginative natures, Chopin
was, in a greater or less degree, according to his state
of health, very superstitious. Loitering along the
Boulevards, one evening after a *soirée*, in company
with some friends, among them A. Szmitkowski, to
whom he dedicated his glorious mazurkas, op. 59, he
was joking about his financial troubles. "I wish,"
he said, "that some good genius would put twenty
thousand francs into my desk. That would set me
up once for all, and I could indulge in the comfort I
am so fond of." That night he dreamt that his
wish was realized. A few days after, on opening a
secret drawer of his desk in which he kept his money
and some much-prized memorials, he actually found
the desired sum. Miss Stirling, his pupil and devoted
follower, had given it to Szmitkowski to put there,
after having heard from him of Chopin's wish and
strange dream.

Chopin had a dislike to the numbers seven and thirteen ; he would never undertake anything of importance on a Monday or Friday, sharing a belief almost universal in Poland that these are unlucky days (ferelne.)

Devoted from childhood to his art, he lived constantly in the tone-world, and when not listening to music, he thought and dreamed of it. It is easy to understand that incessant practice would irritate and chafe his naturally susceptible nerves, and that his feelings, fancies, and even his whole spiritual nature, gradually grew into a state of etherial delicacy. How painful, too, must have been the discord, when he was brought into contact with rough reality. He would then confide to his instrument his inmost thoughts, which became more and more melancholy, until at last his heart broke. Liszt says of Chopin, " To the modern calm simplicity of devotion Chopin united the reverent homage paid to art by the early Mediæval masters. Like them he regarded the exercise of his art as a high and holy calling, and like them too he was proud of having been dedicated by nature to be its priest, and he brought to its service a pious worship which at once ennobles and blesses the artist." These feelings found expression even in his last hours, as a reference to Polish customs will explain. It is still a practice, though less common than formerly, for the dying person to choose the clothes for his burial; many, indeed, have them prepared long beforehand. Thus are

revealed the most secret and cherished thoughts,
and by worldly but believing people the garments of
the cloister are often selected for their last dress,
especially by women. Men are more generally
buried in their uniform with their arms laid beside
them.

Chopin, although not only a composer, but one of
the greatest of pianists (the first of his day as many
think) gave proportionately the fewest concerts; yet
he wished to be laid in the grave in the clothes he
had worn on those occasions. A deep feeling, spring-
ing from the inexhaustible fountain of his artistic
enthusiasm, doubtless prompted this last desire. It
was fulfilled. As he lay covered with flowers and
palm branches in the familiar dress, the admirers
who surrounded his coffin could but exclaim, Frederic
Chopin remained true to himself, for his last thoughts
were of his art.

Banished from his home by political events,
separated from his family, led into the thorny paths
of unhappy love, bowed down by illness, his life was
brought to an early close, but in his sublime creations he has left us a portion of his own rich spirit.

## CHAPTER XIX.

### CHOPIN AS A COMPOSER.

AS a creative artist, Chopin holds a unique position. Confining himself to the comparatively restricted limits of a single instrument, it is, in the opinion of competent judges, his especial merit to have been not only a thoroughly scientific musician, but also a true poet, whose productions have had the most wide-spread influence on all modern pianoforte composers, an influence not unlike that of Heine in the domain of poetry. Poet and musician alike give us the most perfect emotional pictures in the smallest forms, but with this difference, that while Heine's scepticism had a blighting effect on these miniatures, Chopin's harmonious disposition was a fructifying energy. How strongly convinced must Chopin have been that his special mission was the embellishment of pianoforte literature, to be able to resist the tempting and seemingly effective help of an orchestra, and to voluntarily restrict himself to one instrument, for which he wrote master-pieces, of their kind incomparable. Liszt justly observes,

"We are too much accustomed at the present day to consider great only those composers who have, written at least half a dozen Operas and Oratorios, besides Symphonies; demanding, in our folly, everything and more than everything of one musician. However universal this idea may be, its reasonableness is very problematical. We have no wish to contest the hardly won glory or the real superiority of the composers who have adopted the largest forms; all we desire is that, in music, size should be estimated in the same way as in the other arts: a painting, such as the 'Vision of Ezekiel,' or 'The Churchyard,' by Ruysdaël, twenty inches square, is placed among the chefs-d'œuvre, and ranks higher than many larger pictures by a Rubens or a Tintoretto. Is Beranger less of a poet because he poured all his thoughts into the narrow limits of a song? Is not Petrarch known chiefly by his sonnets? How many of his readers are acquainted with his poem on Africa? We cannot but believe that the criticism which denies the superiority of an artist like Schubert over one who occupies himself in scoring tame operatic melodies, will disappear; and that, henceforth, we shall consider the quality of the expression whatever may be the size of the form chosen for its vehicle."

To give a competent analysis of Chopin's works (a list of which with the opus numbers appears at the end of this book) would require a volume to itself. I must, therefore, be content with a general survey of his compositions, enlarging more fully on that species whose origin or, at least, whose high development, we owe to his genius.

The human mind is subject to two kinds of influence—internal and external. The former are determined by natural disposition, the latter by family and national associations. From their union proceeds the individuality of the man who is subject to their ever present forces. Individuality can neither protect its works from influences nor change its own nature, because even if it adopts another course, though the result may be a very perfect organization, the traces of earlier impressions can never be obliterated.

It is interesting to watch the growth and development of Chopin's talents in relation to the different schools. Although under the influence of none in particular, and not following the guide of any of the leading spirits of the day, he showed a slight and brief preference for Hummel, whom he took as a model, especially with regard to his passage work. We can trace this master in the form of most of Chopin's works, while from beginning to end there is an individuality in the choice of thoughts. The leaning to Hummel is chiefly discernible in his rondos ; but in the " Don Juan " variations and the fantasia on Polish airs, that boldness and freshness of thought, independence of working, and originality of conception, which at once gave him a prominent position among contemporary composers, are already apparent. His lavish display of sentiment, youthful grace and energy, hopefulness and melancholy, show how unquenchable were the

springs of his genius. Indeed so vast was the wealth
of his ideas that, as was remarked in referring to his
early works, he never repeated the same thought in
the same manner, but either by the most tasteful
arabesques, or choice changes of harmony, imparted
to it at every return a renewed interest. He was
very clever in turning to account all the embellishments and *fioritures* characteristic of the old Italian
style of vocal music.

Chopin's earliest works are undoubtedly the result
of the musical tendencies of the age; traditional
forms opened to him the gates of the temple where
the greatest masters of pianoforte playing sit en-
throned. But into these forms he infused his own
creative talent. Chopin's imagination struck deeper
chords than that of other composers; he inaugurated
a new era (as he himself wrote to Elsner) and cut a
way for himself, not for the sake of surpassing
others, but by the unconscious impulse of his own
original thoughts. In his youthful years he occasionally availed himself of the resources of the orchestra;
but never afterwards except for the Polonaise, op. 22,
that brilliant piece which, although in E flat major
throughout, begins with a marvellously tender and
imaginative introduction in G major. In the orchestral colouring a certain timidity is frequently
perceptible, owing, perhaps, to an ignorance of the
capacities of the different instruments. He showed
a preference for the violoncello; its elegiac tone was
in harmony with his own nature. Besides the

Y

Polonaise, op. 3, he also composed, with Franchomme, a duet, for piano and 'cello, on motives
from " Robert le Diable " (a work without any
special merit, written in accordance with the taste
of the day), and shortly before his death, the Sonata
in G minor, op. 65, the first movement of which is of
surpassing beauty.

Among the works for piano alone, the Sonatas, as
being his largest compositions, claim our first attention.  The earliest published, as op. 4, dedicated to
Elsner, shows a striving after classic forms, but
does not give us the idea that the composer was
working from inspiration, his wishes and capacities
do not seem always to correspond, and the work
altogether awakens no lasting interest.  The third
movement is most worthy of notice, but this does
not satisfy us completely; it sounds rather forced
and laboured, probably on account of the unusual
$\frac{5}{4}$ measure.  Incomparably more important is the
Sonata in B flat minor, op. 35.  The anxious character of the first theme is happily contrasted with
the exuberant song of the second motive; and the
Funeral March could only have been written by one
in whose soul the pain and mourning of a whole
nation found its echo.

The more dramatic Sonata, in B minor, op. 58, is
better adapted by the brilliancy of its ornamentation
for a concert performance.  The composer seems to
have found it difficult to keep the profusion of
thought within due proportions, especially in the

Adagio. In the development of the first theme in the first movement, there is a want of repose which is only made up for by the wonderful *cantilene* in D major. Chopin is generally less successful when writing in stricter forms which hamper the bold flight of his fancy. His inventive power and melodic wealth were so abundant that it was irksome to him to work out his themes systematically; and his Sonatas, therefore, with respect to form, sometimes appear unfinished; while in more congenial spheres he could permit his rich imagination to have freer play.

Chopin was very partial to the dance forms— mazurka, polonaise, waltz, tarantelle, cracovienne, and bolero—which he first truly idealized. Out of the large number of his mazurkas it is difficult to tell to which to award the palm; so wide a scope do they offer for individual taste. Among the best— which, by their gay or melancholy character, appear so diverse but are all alike characterized by the same rhythm—must undoubtedly be reckoned, op. 7, Nos. 2 and 3; op. 17, Nos. 1 and 2; op. 24, No. 2; op. 30, No. 3; op. 33, No. 4. The mazurkas, op. 24, No. 4; op. 50, No. 3; op. 63, No. 3, distinguished by poetical charm and contrapuntal skill, are worthy of mention. Some of those mazurkas are almost more effective which display a tinge of melancholy, as if the composer had only indulged in a momentary diversion and narcotic intoxication to return the more sadly to his original gloom. The most striking mazurka of this class is op. 56, No. 2.

Tradition assigns to the polonaise the following origin. When the dynasty of the Jagiellons died out, Henry of Anjou, son of Catherine de Medicis, afterwards Henry III., was, in 1573, elected King of Poland. The following year he received the representatives of the nation in solemn state at Cracow Castle; and the gentlemen made their wives slowly defile before the king, keeping step to an accompaniment of music. Every time a foreign prince was elected to the throne this ceremony was repeated, and from it was gradually developed the national dance of the polonaise, which has kept its place in Europe up to the present day. In the slow sweeping measure of the polonaise there is much stateliness and gravity, and the turnings and changes seem like the echo of the murmurs from the active life of the old Polish nobility. It used always to be danced with the sabre called "Carabella." Prince Michael Oginski and afterwards Kurpinski were the first to treat it artistically, a circumstance which contributed in some measure to their reputation; after them, non-Polish composers, such as Beethoven, Schubert, Weber, Spohr, &c., made it into an independent musical form, and wrote works on the model of the polonaise; until Chopin ennobled it with his own poetry and ideal beauty, and once more infused into it a distinctively Polish cast of thought.

Chopin's polonaises may be divided into two groups: the one with its marked rhythm, displaying the martial element; the other the dreamy melancholy feeling peculiar to Chopin. To the first order I should assign the polonaises in A major, op. 40, No. 1; F sharp minor, op. 44; and A flat major, op. 53. For simplicity of form and characteristic nationality the preference must be given to the polonaise in A major; although technically inferior and deficient in poetry—for it is *forte* almost throughout, and the themes are not well contrasted—it is effective on account of its chivalric ring and natural dignity. The grandest and boldest is undoubtedly the F sharp minor polonaise, dedicated to Princess Beauvau, sister to Countess Delphine Potocka. The gloomy colouring and wildly defiant character of the chief theme are suddenly interrupted by a charming *intermezzo* in the mazurka style. Almost equally marvellous is the dreamy *finale*, in which, while the right hand holds the C sharp—to which the semitone D immediately falls like a heavy *appoggiatura*—in the left hand the energetic theme dies away to the gentlest *pianissimo*. The majestic A flat major polonaise was composed in 1840 after Chopin's return from Majorca.

Chopin's nervous system was so much affected by his illness that, for sometime afterwards, his restless imagination would not permit him to sleep. One night, while playing a work he had just finished, he fancied that the doors opened, and that a great company of Polish knights and noble ladies in the old costume (robe ronde et cornettes) came in and

marched past him. He was so much perturbed
by this vision that he rushed out through the opposite
door and would not return to his room for the rest
of the night. Indeed the middle movement in E
major, with the long crescendo in the bass, so
vividly conjures up an approaching band of knights,
galloping over a plain in the pale light of the moon
that one hears in fancy the tramp of the fiery steeds
and the clatter of arms.

The second group comprises the polonaises in
C sharp and E flat minor, op. 26; the polonaise
in C minor, op. 40, No. 2; and three in D minor,
B flat major, and F minor, op. 71, published by
Fontana. The two first, dedicated to J. Dessauer,
are pre-eminent for loftiness of sentiment. They
were composed at a time when Chopin was at the
summit of his greatness, when his vigorous and
original mind, unhampered by trivial considerations
about form, created for itself the form best adapted
to its conceptions. For example, the first polonaise
(C sharp minor) not only has a melody of uncommon
beauty, but there is also a rare depth of character
in the apparently bold incoherent themes with
which the work begins. While the grand rhythmical
swing of the first theme depicts manly courage,
which is tempered by an erotic love theme, the
second subject, with the exception of the lightning-
like passages in the right hand, is of a hopeful,
soothing character; the D flat major motive closes
the happy scene. None of the later polonaises

contain a double motion of the melody, as we find
in the conclusion of this.   The second number
of the same opus (E flat minor) is mysterious,
gloomy, and shuddering; it seems to picture the
suffering Poles banished in chains to Siberia.

The Fantasie-polonaise in A flat major, op. 61,
holds a position distinct from either of these groups.
It is intended to represent the national struggles
and contests, and concludes, therefore, with a pom-
pous hymn of victory.   Chopin's firm belief in the
ultimate triumph of the Polish nation after its
many bitter trials—a feeling so well depicted in
the poetry of Mickiewicz, Krasinski, and frequently
of Slowacki, the greatest poets of that period—
speaks out very clearly in this the most finished
of his larger pianoforte works.

It would be foolish to seek in Music for allegory,
history, politics, or philosophical deductions.   The
sphere of music is feeling, through which and to
which it speaks, and through feeling unites itself
with the poetry of the present day, not only by
a common national sentiment, but in nearly all
its tones and *nuances*. Chopin's music is like poetry,
a flower of Romanticism, and it has the same
beauties and the same defects as our romantic
poetry.   It touches the highest and deepest springs
of emotion, is original, rich in thoughts and forms;
but it suffers from the same exaggerated sentiment
and melancholy, and frequently degenerates into
nervous debility.

Chopin's waltzes (op. 18, 34, 42, 64, 69, and 70), partly because they are the least technically difficult, partly on account of the popularity of this dance form, have become most widely known. Musically considered, they offer less of interest and novelty than his other compositions. What they lose in the rhythm of the dance they gain in innate grace and outward brilliancy, such as no composer hitherto had been able to impart to this form. The most interesting are those which are pervaded by that peculiar melancholy, "schwärmerisch" vein, which is one of the chief charms of Chopin's muse. Such are the waltzes in A minor and C sharp minor, the latter inclining in the third and fourth bar to the mazurka measure, for which Chopin always showed a preference.

The four ballads (op. 23, 38, 47, and 52), are among the finest and most original of his works. They contain so much that is new and varied in form that critics long hesitated to what category they should assign them. Some regarded them as a variety of the rondo; others, with more accuracy, called them "poetical stories." Indeed, there is about them a narrative tone (märchenton) which is particularly well rendered by the $\frac{6}{4}$ and $\frac{6}{8}$ time, and which makes them differ essentially from the existing forms. Chopin himself said to Schumann, on the occasion of their meeting at Leipsic, that he had been incited to the creation of the ballads by some poems of Mickiewicz. The first and perhaps the best known in G minor, op. 23, is inflamed by wild passion, and claims special admiration for its finish of detail, the second and third have a predominantly idyllic character. The fourth, and technically the most difficult, is, perhaps, for this reason the least known. The critics who, with the exception of Robert Schumann, unanimously condemned Chopin's larger works, made a fierce onslaught on this ballad. But, in my opinion, this displays the most poetry and intelligence of them all; and, for a satisfactory interpretation of its manifold beauties, not only considerable mechanical skill, but also subtle musical perception are required.

The nocturnes appear, at first sight, to have most affinity with forms already created. Field, for a long time erroneously looked upon as Chopin's master, was the author of this form; but the difference of treatment by the two masters is apparent in its very likeness. Field was satisfied with writing tender, poetical, and rather melancholy pieces; while Chopin not only introduced the dramatic element, but displayed, in a striking manner, a marvellous enrichment of harmony and of the resources of pianoforte composition. Compare, for example, Chopin's E flat major nocturne, op. 9, with Field's, in B flat major, and the broad difference is at once perceived. Among Chopin's best productions of this kind are the nocturne, op. 15, No. 2 (in doppio movimento); the beautiful D flat major nocturne, op. 27, with its profusion of delicate *fioritures ;* and also the one in G minor, op. 37, which keeps up a ceaseless moan, as if harping on some sad thought, until interrupted by a church-like movement in chords whose sadly comforting strains resemble the peacefulness of the grave. The following nocturne, op. 37, No. 2, contains in the middle movement, perhaps the most beautiful melody Chopin ever wrote, to which one can never listen without a sense of the deepest emotion and happiness. Op. 48, No. 1, in C minor, is broad and most imposing with its powerful intermediate movement, which is a thorough departure from the nocturne style. The nocturne, published posthumously as op. 72, was written in 1827, and bears evident traces of that youthful period; op. 62, No. 2, in E major, was written shortly before Chopin's death, and is full of refinements of harmony, sweet melody, and reverie.

Almost the same thing may be said of the scherzi as of the ballads : they did not exist before Chopin, or at least not in the same measure of independence, daring boldness, and almost Shaksperian humour. In the most well-known of these in B flat minor, op. 31, the first theme is obstinately gloomy, yet not despondent but defiant; and scarcely less fine is the clever and expressive second subject in A major. To appreciate to the full Chopin's creative powers his pianoforte pieces must be compared with those of his contemporaries, for the scherzi still appear so modern that it might well be said they were thirty years in advance of their time.

In demonianism and drastic power the B flat minor scherzo, op. 31, resembles those in B minor, op. 20, and in C sharp minor, op. 39 ; while the one in E minor, op. 54, presents a kindlier face. The rhythm of the scherzi, far more than of the mazurkas, expresses a certain spirited opposition, a fascinating arrogance; and as the dance forms to which the mazurkas and polonaises in part still belonged were completely destroyed by the middle theme, the specimens of the scherzo may be regarded as a wonderfully true expression of Chopin's courageous individuality, decisive both outwardly and inwardly, noble, amiable, and poetic.

The preludes (op. 28 and 45) and the four impromptus (op. 29, 36, 51, and 66) show a slight leaning towards the nocturnes—as, for example, the unhappily little known but richly modulated prelude in C sharp minor, op. 45 ; also the D flat major, op. 28, No. 15, with a splendid middle movement in C sharp minor, and the impromptu in F sharp major, op. 36—and partake partly of the nature of a study —as, for example, the impromptus in A flat major and G flat major, with their melodious middle movements ; and the preludes, op. 28, Nos. 1, 3, 8, 16, 19, and 23—and are also in part hasty sketches in which the composer, in spite of the smallness of their dimensions, gives us the most clever imaginative pictures. Some of them—such as those in E

minor and B minor—are real gems, and would alone
suffice to immortalize the name of Chopin as a poet.

Chopin deserves especial honour for having per-
fected the study. Some of his studies (op. 10, 25,
and " Trois Nouvelles Etudes,") serve purely technical purposes, such as op. 10, Nos. 1, 2, 4, 8 ; op. 25,
Nos. 6, 8, and No. 3 of the " Trois Nouvelles
Etudes ; " others are important intellectually, such
as op. 10, Nos. 3, 9, 10, 12 ; op. 25, Nos. 1 and 7 ;
and No. 1 of the " Etudes."

The works which Fontana published at Schles-
inger's after Chopin's death—Fantasie-impromptu,
op. 66 : quatre mazurkas, op. 67 ; quatre mazurkas,
op. 68 ; deux valses, op. 69 ; trois valses, op. 70 ;
trois polonaises, op. 71 ; nocturne, marche funèbre,
trois ecossaises, op. 72 ; rondeau pour deux pianos,
op. 73 ; sixteen Polish songs, op. 74—are, with the
exception of a few such, as op. 66, which are well
worthy of the name of their composer, of less musical
value. Chopin wished them to be destroyed after
his death, or at least not published. The last
mazurka, *senza fine*, composed a few days before he
died, is sad, very sad, like the last days of the great
master. He showed by this swan-song and by his
yearning after the home of his happy youth, that in
the very last hour of his creative inspiration he remained faithful to his national music and to his
sorely-tried fatherland.

The sixteen Polish songs were written without any
titles. If he met with any new and beautiful poetry

in his native tongue, he would set it to music, not for publication but for his own pleasure. Thus these songs gradually accumulated between 1824 and 1844. Many have been lost because, in spite of the requests of his friends, the composer constantly put off committing them to paper; others were sung in Poland without anything positive being known as to their origin, but it is pretty certainly conjectured that Chopin was their composer. Among these must be mentioned the popular and formerly much sung " The third of May."

Unimportant in a musical point of view, it could not be expected that they would be diffused beyond the confines of Poland. They sprang from the seed of the later national poetical growth, scattered as if by accident on Chopin's receptive soul; they are simple flowers which do not dazzle, but by their sweet perfume and peculiar delicacy delight sympathetic hearts.

# APPENDIX.

### EIGHT MORE LETTERS OF CHOPIN TO TITUS WOYCIECHOWSKI.

SUBJOIN a few letters written by Chopin between 1828 and 1831 to his friend Titus Woyciechowski, which I did not think it necessary to insert in the biography :—

### I.

*Warsaw, Saturday, December 27th, 1828.*

MY DEAREST FRIEND,

Hitherto I have delayed writing to you, but now friendship triumphs over idleness, and, sleepy as I am, I take up my pen that you may have this in time for the 1st and the 4th of January. I do not desire to fill my letter with compliments, good wishes, or trite jokes, for we both understand each other perfectly—whence my silence and the laconic nature of this epistle. . . . .

The score of my Rondo Cracovienne is ready. The introduction is almost as funny as I am in my great coat,*

---

* A very long winter overcoat, made by Boy, in which his friends said he cut a very comical figure.

and the trio is not quite finished. My parents have just had fitted up for me a little room, leading by a staircase direct from the *entree*; there will be an old *secrétaire* in it, and I shall make it my den. That orphan child, the Rondo for two pianos, has found a step-father in Fontana, (whom you may, perhaps, have seen here; he goes to the University); he has learnt it after a month's study, and, a short time ago, we tried it over at Buchholtz's to see how it might sound. I say "might," for the instruments were not tuned alike, and our fingers were stiff, so we could have no adequate impression of the effect of the work. For a week past I have composed nothing of any value. I run from Ananias to Caiaphas; this evening I was at Madame Wizegerod's, and from there went to a musical *soirée* at Mlle. Kicka's. You know how pleasant it is to be pressed to improvise when you are tired. I seldom now have such happy thoughts as when you were with me. And then the wretched instruments one finds everywhere. I have not found one either in mechanism or tone anything approaching ours or your sister's.

The Polish theatre opened yesterday with " Preciosa." The French have given " Rataplan ;" to-day, the " Geldhab," by Fredro ; and to-morrow, Auber's " Maurer und Schlosser" are to be performed. Somebody or other said to me the other day that you had written to him. Do not think I am angry with you for not having written to me for so long ; I know you well enough, and do not think anything of a bit of paper; I should not have scribbled so much nonsense to-day, but to remind you that you still hold the same place in my heart, and that I am the same Fritz as ever. You do not like being kissed,

but you must put up with it to-day.  We all unite
in best wishes to your mother.  Zywny sends warmest
remembrances.

Your FREDERIC.

II.

*Warsaw, April 10th, 1830.*

*(Anniversary of Emily's death.)*

I have been vainly wishing to write to you for some
weeks past.  I don't know why the time should pass so
quickly now.  Our musical season is at its height,
Passion week even was disregarded.  Last Monday
there was a grand *soirée* at Philippeus's, when Madame
Saurin sang a duet from " Semiramis " very beautifully ;
I accompanied Messrs. Soliva and Gresser in a Buffo
Duet from Rossini's "Turk in Italy," which, by unan-
imous desire, was repeated.  I have sketched out a
programme of the *soirée* at Lewicki's, at which Prince
Galizin is to take part in a quartet by Rode.  I shall
select Hummel's " La Sentinelle," and shall finish with
my polonaise with violoncello, to which I have written
an Adagio by way of introduction.  I have tried it
already, it does not go badly.  This is the latest *salon*
news, and now for the newspaper intelligence, which is
no less important to me, as it includes some most
favourable opinions about myself.  I should like to send
them to you.  There was an article, two pages long, in
the *Warsaw Gazette,* in which Elsner was very much
abused.  Soliva told me that he only avoided the controversy because two of his pupils were shortly to make

a public appearance, otherwise he should certainly have replied to the attack. It is difficult to describe the whole case in a few words; I would send you the newspaper if I could, so as to make the matter quite clear. A word to the wise is sufficient, so I will give a brief outline of the affair.

My concerts called forth a great many laudatory notices, especially in the *Polish Courier*, and the *Official Journal* also gave me a few words of praise. This was all very well, but one of the numbers of the latter newspaper, although in perfect good faith, was full of such absurdities that I felt quite in despair until I read in the *Gazette Polska* a refutation of the exaggerated statements in the *Official Journal*. This paper was mad enough to say that Poland would one day be as proud of me as Germany is of Mozart; and that " if I had fallen into the hands of a pedant or a Rossinist (what a ridiculous expression!) I should never have been what I am." Although, indeed, I am nothing yet, the critic is so far right in saying that if I had not studied with Elsner, I should have done still less. This taunt at a Rossinist, and praise of Elsner made somebody so angry* that, in an article in the *Warsaw Gazette*, beginning with Fredro's comedy, "Die Freunde," and ending with "Grafen Ory," there was the following paragraph : " Why should any gratitude be due to Elsner? he does not make pupils off hand," and (at my second concert Nowakowski's symphony was performed) " the Devil even cannot make something out of nothing."

---

* The bandmaster Kurpinski, who because he gave scarcely any operas but Rossini's, was often called a Rossinist. There is no doubt that he wrote the anonymous article referred to.

z

Thirty-five years ago Elsner wrote a quartet, to which
the publisher, without the author's knowledge, appended
the title " Dans le meilleur gout polonais," on account of
the Polish character of the Menuet. The present
reviewer, without mentioning the composer's name,
ridicules this quartet. Soliva says truly that they would
have been just as much justified in abusing " Caecilia,"*
especially as, with all kindness and delicacy, they give
me some side thrusts, and the good piece of advice that
I should listen to Rossini but not copy him. No doubt
this was said because the other article remarked that I
had a great deal of originality.

I am invited to an Easter breakfast at Minasowicz's †
for the day after to-morrow; Kurpinski is to be there,
and I am very curious to see how he will behave towards
me. You would not believe how amiable he always is
to me. I saw him last Wednesday week at little Leskie-
wicz's concert. The latter does not play badly, although
he still shows that he is a learner. It seems to me that
he will be a better player than Krogulski, but I have not
yet ventured to say so, though I have been often asked
for an opinion.

Oh! the postman! A letter . . . . . from you!
Oh, my dear friend, how good you are! It is no wonder,
however, for I am always thinking of you. As far as I
can gather from your letter, you have only seen the
*Warsaw Courier;* get the *Polish Courier*, and No. 91 of
the *Warsaw Gazette*, if you can. Your advice is good;
I had already given up some invitations for the evening

---

* A Polish national opera by Kurpinski.
† A Polish poet, died 1849.

as if in anticipation of it, for I always think a great deal of you in everything that I undertake. I do not know whether it is because I have learnt to think and feel with you, but when I write anything I always want to know if it pleases you, and my second concerto (E minor) will not have any value in my eyes until you have heard and approved it.

My third concert, which is being counted on here, will not take place until shortly before I leave; I think of playing the new Concerto, which is not yet finished, then, by desire, the Fantasia on Polish airs, and the Variations dedicated to you, which I am anxiously awaiting, as the Leipsic fair has already begun, and Brzezina has received a large consignment of music. The Frenchman from St. Petersburg, who wanted to treat me with champagne after my second concert, and whom people took for Field, is a pupil from the Paris Conservatoire, named Dunst. He has given several concerts in St. Petersburg, which made a great sensation, so he must play unusually well. You will, doubtless, think it strange, a Frenchman from St. Petersburg with a German name. I have the sad piece of news to add that Orlowski has been making mazurkas and galops on my themes; but I have begged him not to have them printed.

### III.

*Warsaw, April 17th,* 1830.
*(Papa's birth-day.)*

A letter from you gives me some respite from my unendurable yearning (sehnsucht), and to-day I was

more than ever in need of this consolation. I want
to drive away the thoughts which poison my happiness;
yet, it gives me pleasure to dally with them; I do not
know what ails me . . . . perhaps I shall be calmer by
the end of this letter.

I am very pleased to hear that there is some pro-
bability of your coming, for I am going to remain until
the meeting of the Diet, which, as you have doubtless
seen by the newspapers, will take place on the 28th inst.,
and last a month. The *Warsaw Courier* has already
announced the arrival of Mlle. Sonntag; Dmuszewski,
the editor, is incorrigible, he is always getting hold
of some story, which he prefixes by saying, "We learn,
on good authority," &c., &c. When I met him yesterday
he told me that he was going to insert a sonnet addressed
to me. I begged him, for heaven's sake, not to do anything so absurd. "It is already printed," he replied,
with a smile, thinking that I should feel very much
delighted and honoured. Oh, these mistaken favours!
Those who envy me will have another mark to shoot
at. With regard to the mazurkas on themes from my
Concerto, mercenary motives have won the day, and
they are already published. I do not care to read
anything more that people may write about me.

Last week I had an idea of coming to see you, but
was too busy; I must work as hard as I can to finish
my compositions. If you come to Warsaw for the
meeting of the Diet, you will be at my concert. I have
a presentiment that you will, and if I dream that you do,
I shall firmly believe it.* How often do I turn night

---

* Another instance of Chopin's inclination to superstition.

into day, and day into night; how often do I wake in
dreams, and sleep in the day; but it is not like sleep, for
I always feel the same, and instead of gaining refresh-
ment, I worry myself, and rack my brains, till I am quite
exhausted.

Pray think kindly of me  .  .  .  .

## IV.

*Warsaw, June 5th,* 1830.

MY DEAR FRIEND,

You have missed five of Mlle. Sonntag's concerts,
but if you come on the 13th, you will have several
opportunities of hearing her. The 13th will be Sunday,
and you will arrive just when I am at home, trying over
the Allegro of the Second Concerto, as I am making all
the use I can of Mlle. Sonntag's absence. I learnt from
her own pretty lips that she was going to Fischbach,* by
invitation from the King of Prussia, and that she would
return from there to us.

I cannot tell you what pleasure I have received from
closer acquaintance with this " heavenly messenger," as
some enthusiasts justly call her; I am sincerely grateful
to Prince Anton Radziwill for having introduced me. I,
unfortunately, got but little benefit from her week's stay
here, for she was bored with wearisome visits from
senators, Woiewodes, castellans, ministers, generals,
and adjutants, who sat staring at her and making dull
speeches. She received them all very kindly, for she is

---

* A castle of the King of Prussia, beautifully situated at the
foot of the Riesengebirge.

too good-hearted to be ever unamiable. Yesterday,
when she wanted to go out to a rehearsal, she was
actually obliged to shut herself up in her room, as the
servant could not keep the hosts of callers out of the
ante-room. I should not have gone to her had she not
sent for me, on account of Radziwill having asked me to
write out a song he had arranged for her. It consists of
variations on an Ukrainian folk-song (Dumka); the theme
and the *finale* are pretty, but I do not at all like the middle
movement, and Mlle. Sonntag approves of it still less; I
have made some alterations, but it won't do yet. I am
glad that she is going after to-day's concert, as I shall
thus be released from this trouble, and when Radziwill
comes back for the close of the Diet, he will, perhaps,
have given up his variations.

Mlle. Sonntag is not beautiful, but extremely fascinating; everyone is enchanted with her voice, which is
not particularly powerful, but splendidly cultivated. Her
*diminuendo* is the *non plus ultra*, her *portamento* wonderfully beautiful, and her chromatic scales, in the
upper register especially, unequalled. She sang us
an air by Mercadente very beautifully, and Rode's
variations, especially the last *roulades*, more than
excellently. The variations on a Swiss theme were
so much liked that she was obliged, after repeatedly
bowing her acknowledgments, to sing them *da capo;*
and the same thing occurred yesterday after the last
variation by Rode. She sang also the Cavatina from
the "Barbier," and some airs from the "Diebischen
Elster" and the "Freischütz." But soon you will be able
to judge for yourself of the difference between her
performances and anything that we have heard here

before. One day when I was with her, Soliva brought
Mlles. Gladkowska and Wolkow to sing to her their duet,
closing with the words " barbara sorte " (you remember
it, do you not?) Mlle. Sonntag said to me, in confidence,
that both voices were very beautiful, but rather screamy,
and that the young ladies must change their method
of singing altogether, unless they wanted to run the
risk of losing their voices completely in two years.
I heard her say to Mlle. Wolkow that she sang with a
great deal of ease and taste, but had " une voix trop
aigue." She invited them both in the kindest manner
to come and see her more often, and promised to spare
no pains to teach them her own method. Is not that
a rare piece of politeness? Indeed, I believe it was
exquisite coquetry which made on me the impression
of *naïveté ;* for one can scarcely imagine anyone
being so natural unless acquainted with all the arts of
coquetry.

Mlle. Sonntag is a hundred times prettier and nicer *en
deshabille* than in evening dress, but those who have only
seen her in the concert room are charmed with her beautiful appearance. On her return she will give concerts
until the 22nd instant, when, she tells me, she thinks of
going to St. Petersburg. So make haste, dear friend,
and come at once that you may not miss any more
concerts.

There is a good deal of talk about Pasta coming, and
of both the artists singing together. A French lady
pianist, Mlle. Belleville, is here, and intending to give
a concert next Wednesday ; her playing is very good,
very light and elegant, ten times better than Worlitzer's.
She took part in the famous " soirée musicale " at the

Court, when Sonntag sang and Worlitzer played, though without giving much satisfaction, as I heard from Kurpinski, who accompanied the great vocalist. A good many people were surprised (*not* including myself) that I was not invited to play. . . . . But some more about Mlle. Sonntag. There is a great deal of new *broderie* in her execution, which is very effective, but not so much so as Paganini's; perhaps because it is of a smaller kind. She seems to bring with her the perfume of a fresh bouquet, and to caress and play with her voice, but she rarely moves one to tears. Radziwill, however, thinks that her impersonation of Desdemona, in the last scene of " Otello," is such that no one could refrain from weeping.

I asked her, early this morning, if she would not give us this scene in costume (for she is a capital actress); she replied that although she could move an audience to tears, yet acting affected her so painfully that she had determined to appear on the stage as seldom as possible.

Come here to rest yourself from your rural cares; when you hear Mlle. Sonntag sing you will wake up to new life and gather fresh strength for your work. What a pity I cannot send myself instead of this letter . . . . Mlle. Belleville has played my Variations, published in Vienna; she knows one of them by heart. To-day Mlle. Sonntag will sing something from " Semiramis." Her concerts are short, she sings at the utmost four times, the orchestra playing between. Indeed one needs to rest after her singing, so powerful an impression does it produce and so interesting is she as an artist.

## V.

*Warsaw, (I think) September 4th, 1830.*

My ideas are growing more and more confused. I am here still, and cannot make up my mind to fix definitively a day for my departure. It seems to me as if I were leaving Warsaw for ever; I have a presentiment that I am bidding an eternal farewell to my home. Oh, how hard it must be to die anywhere but in one's birth-place. How could I bear to see around my death-bed, instead of the faces of my beloved family, an unconcerned doctor and a hired servant. Believe me, dear Titus, I often long to come to you to ease my heavy heart, but as I cannot do that I rush out of doors without knowing why. But that does not calm or satisfy my restless, yearning spirit, and I go home only to sigh again . . . .

I have not yet tried my Concerto. At any rate I shall have left my treasure behind me before Michaelmas.* In Vienna I shall be condemned to eternal sighs and languishing. This is so when one's heart is no longer free. You know very well what that is, but can you account for that peculiar feeling which makes people always expect something better from the morrow? " Do not be so foolish," is all the answer I can give myself; if you know a better one, pray, pray tell it me . . .

These are my plans for the winter: I think of staying two months in Vienna; then going to Italy and perhaps spending the winter in Milan. Soliva always conducts the operas in which his pupils appear; in time, I think,

---

* A reference to his attachment to Mlle. Gladkowska.

he will unseat Kurpinski ; he has one foot in the stirrup already, and is supported by a doughty cavalier.*

I finish my letter to-day with nothing, indeed with less than nothing, that is with what I have already said before. It is half-past eleven, and I am still sitting here *en deshabille*, although Mariolka will certainly be already waiting to go with me to dinner at C.'s. I have promised to visit Magnuszewski afterwards, so I shall not be back before four o'clock to finish the page, and the sight of the blank paper annoys me.

But I will not worry myself unnecessarily, or I shall never come to an end, and Mariolka will be disappointed altogether ; and, as you know, I like to make myself agreeable to people of whose good-will I am assured. I have not been to see her since my return, and I must confess that I often blame her as the cause of my dejection ; other people seem to be of the same opinion, and this gives me at last some slight satisfaction. My father smiles, but if he knew all I think he would weep. I seem quite happy, but my heart. . . . .

By this day month you will have no more letters from Warsaw, nor perhaps from anywhere else ; perhaps you will not hear from me again before we meet. I am writing nothing but nonsense now ; only the thought of leaving Warsaw . . . .

Bnt wait awhile, and perhaps you will yourself be no better off. Man is never always happy, and very often only a brief period of happiness is granted him in

---

* General Rozniecki, who was then president of the National Theatre.

this world; so why escape from this dream which cannot last long?

If I sometimes regard intercourse with the world as a, sacred duty, at other times, I consider it a devilish invention, and that it would be better if mankind . . . but enough . . . Time flies, and I must wash . . . don't kiss me yet . . . but you would not kiss me even if I were anointed with Byzantian oil, unless by some magnetism I forced you to. Farewell.

## VI.

*Warsaw, September 18th, 1830.*

I don't know exactly why I am still here, but I am very happy, and my parents agree to my remaining. Last Wednesday, I tried my concerto with quartet accompaniment, but was not quite satisfied with it. Those who were present at the rehearsal say that the *finale* is the most successful movement—perhaps because it is the most easily understandable. I shall not be able to tell you till next week how it will sound with the full orchestra, as I am not going to try it until Wednesday. To-morrow I am going to have another rehearsal with the quartet accompaniment, and then I shall go— whither? I have no special attraction anywhere, but at any rate I shall not stay in Warsaw. If you imagine that some beloved object keeps me here you are wrong, like a good many other people. I can assure you that as far as I am concerned, I am ready for any sacrifice. I love, but I must keep my unhappy passion locked in my own breast for some years longer. I do not want to start with you, for the sake of the pleasure of meeting;

the moment when we embrace for the first time on a foreign soil will be more precious to me than a thousand days of travelling together.

I intended to write a polonaise with orchestral accompaniment; but have only sketched it out in my head; when it will see the light I cannot say. The *Wiener Zeitung* contains a good critique on my variations, short but comprehensive, and so philosophical that it is almost impossible to translate. The writer concludes by saying that the work has not only an external beauty, but an intrinsic excellence, which will defy the changes of fashion and make it last for ever. That is indeed a handsome compliment, for which I shall thank the reviewer when I see him. I am very pleased with the article, because, while it is not at all exaggerated, it acknowledges my independence. I should not say so much to any one but you, but we understand each other so well, that I may venture, like the merchants, to praise my own wares.

Orlowski's new ballet is to be given to-day for the first time. There is more talk about the astounding nature of the spectacle than the originality of the music. I was at great big C.'s yesterday, for his name-day, when I played in Spohr's Quintet for piano, clarionet, bassoon, French horn, and flute.* The work is wonderfully beautiful, but the pianoforte part not very playable. Everything that Spohr wrote for the piano is very difficult, and for many of his passages one cannot find any fingering at all. Instead of commencing at 7 o'clock, we did not begin playing until eleven. You are, doubtless, surprised

---

* Chopin places the instruments in this order.

that I was not fast asleep. But there was a very good reason why I should not be, for among the guests was a beautiful girl, who vividly reminded me of my ideal. Just fancy, I stayed till 3 a.m.

I was to have started for Vienna by the Cracow diligence this day week, but finally gave up the idea,— you can guess why. You may rest assured that I am no egoist, and as truly as I love you, would make any sacrifice for other people. For other people, I say, but not for outside appearance; for public opinion, which has great weight here, although I am not much influenced by it, regards it as a misfortune for a man to have a shabby coat, or a rubbed hat. If I do not succeed in my profession, and wake up some fine morning to find that I have nothing to eat, you must get a clerkship for me at Poturzyn.* I shall be as happy in a stable as I was in your castle last summer. As long as I have health and strength I will gladly work all my days. I have often thought it over whether I was really lazy, or whether I could do more without physical injury. Joking apart, I am quite sure that I am not very lazy yet, and that, if necessary, I could do double what I do.

People often lose the good opinion of others by trying to gain it; but I do not think that I shall either raise or lower myself in your estimation, although I do sing my own praises, for there is mutual sympathy between us. You are not master of your thoughts, but I can command mine, and when I get an idea into my head, I will not part with it, any more than the trees will allow themselves to be robbed of the green covering which is the

---

* Mons. Woyciechowski's estate, where he is still living.

charm and beauty of their life. I, too, keep gréen in winter, though only in the head, my heart is red-hot, so it is no wonder the vegetation is so luxuriant. May God help me? Enough . . Yours for ever . . I have just discovered what nonsense I have been talking. You see I have not got over the effects of yesterday, have not had my sleep out, and am still tired with having danced four mazurkas! Your letters are tied up with a ribbon given me by my ideal. I am very glad that two inanimate things agree together so well; it is probably because, although they do not know each other, they both feel that they come from hands dear to me.

------

## VII.

*Warsaw, September 22nd, 1830.*

I must first explain how it is I am still here. For a fortnight past my father has objected to my going on account of the disturbances throughout Germany; in the Rhine provinces, Darmstadt, Brunswick, Capel, and Saxony, where the new king has already ascended the throne. It is reported here that there are riots in Vienna about the meal business; I don't know what it is they want, but it is certain they are fighting over it. There are agitations also in the Tyrol, while in Italy they are ready to boil over, and we expect to hear something important every minute. I have not yet inquired about a pass, but it is thought that I shall only get one for Austria or Prussia; Italy and France are not to be thought of, and I know that some, and often all, passports have been refused. I shall probably go to Vienna in a few weeks, *via* Cracow, for I am remembered there, and one must strike while the iron is hot.

P. was with me yesterday; he starts early to-morrow, and as I am going to have a rehearsal of my second Concerto to-day, with full orchestra (except trumpets and kettledrums), I have invited him to it, for your sake. He will be able to tell you all about it, and I know that the smallest particulars will interest you. I am very sorry that you are not here; Kurpinski, Soliva, and the *élite* of the musical world will be present, but, with the exception of course of Elsner, I have not much confidence in their judgment. I am most curious to know what the band-master will think of the Italian; Czapek of Kessler; Philippeus of Dobrzynski; Molsdorf of Kaczynski; Ledoux of Soltyk; and Mons. P. of us all. No one has ever assembled all these gentlemen in one place before; I do it out of curiosity.

I am very sorry I have to write on a day like this when I cannot compose myself. It almost drives me out of my mind to think about myself, and I often go about so buried in thought as to be in danger of being run over, which, indeed, nearly happened yesterday. Catching a glimpse of my ideal in church, I rushed out in a state of happy stupefaction, and it was nearly a quarter of an hour before I came to myself again. I am quite frightened sometimes at my own distraction. I should like to send you a few trifles I have just composed, but don't know whether I shall manage to write them out to-day.

I beg you to excuse this hasty letter, but I must hasten off to Elsner to make sure of his presence at the rehearsal. Then I must see about the desks, and the *sordini*, which I quite forgot yesterday, but without which the *adagio* would be nothing. The *rondo* is

effective, and the first *allegro* powerful. Confounded
self-love! But if anyone is responsible for my share
of it, it is you. You egoist, who could live with a
person like you without growing like you? However,
in one respect I am still unlike: I can never make a
rapid resolution. Still, I have relentlessly determined
on departing next Saturday week, in spite of any amount
of weeping and lamentation. The music in the trunk,
the familiar ribbon on my heart, a mind full of care, and
I am off in the post carriage. Of course the city will
flow with tears from Copernicus to the fountain, and
from the bank to King Sigismund's column; but I shall
be as cold and insensible as a stone, and laugh at all the
people who want to take such a tender adieu of me. . .

## VIII.

*Paris, December 25th, 1831.*

For the second time, my dear Titus, I have to send
my birth-day congratulations from a long, long distance.
A look, a pressure of the hand would say more than a
dozen letters, so I will not waste many words. I cannot
write *ex abrupto*, and I have not yet bought one of the
books of congratulations which the boys are shrieking
about the streets at two sous a copy. The Parisians are a
strange people; towards evening you hear nothing but the
names of new books, which consist of three or four pages
of printed nonsense. The youngsters push their wares so
well, that in the end, whether you will or no, you are sure
to lay out a sou or two. The following are some specimens
of the titles, " l'art de faire des amours et de les con-
server ensuite;" "les amours des prêtres;" "l'Arche-
veque de Paris avec Madame la duchesse de Berry," and

hundreds of like absurdities, which are, however, often very wittily written. It is really astonishing what means are resorted to for earning a penny, for there is a great deal of distress in Paris just now, and money is scarce, There are a good many shabby, desperate looking men about, and one over-hears some threatening talk about Louis Philippe and his ministry only hanging by a hair. The populace are enraged against the Government, and would like to overthrow it, for the sake of putting an end to the misery abroad; but the latter are too much on their guard, and the smallest crowd is dispersed by the mounted gendarmerie. You must know that I am living on the fourth floor, but in one of the boulevards in the best part of Paris. I have a balcony over-looking the street, and so have a good view right and left over the moving masses. General Ramorino has taken up his quarters exactly opposite in the Cité bergère.*

You know, of course, how the Germans everywhere received him, how in Strasburg the French dragged his carriage in triumph through the streets; in short, you know all about the enthusiasm of the populace for our

---

Girolamo Ramorino, illegitimate son of Marshal Lannes, was born in Genoa, 1792; he left his country for political reasons, and entered the French army, to take part in the war against Austria and Russia. During the Restoration he lived in Savoy. When the revolution broke out in Piedmont in 1821, he bravely and successfully commanded the insurgent forces. When the disturbances were over he went to France, and in 1830, to Warsaw, when he became colonel in the Polish army. He distinguished himself in several battles and soon obtained the rank of General. At the end of August, 1831, he was ordered to lead 20,000 men against the Russian general, Rosen, on the right bank of the Vistula, and to victual

A A

general. Paris did not wish to be behind in this respect.
The " école de médecine" and the "jeune France," who
wear beards and neckties after a certain pattern, arranged
for a grand demonstration. The ultra sections of every
political party have their peculiar badge : the Carlists
wear green waistcoats; the Republicans, Napoleonists,
(these include "la jeune France") and the Simonists,
who profess a new religion, and have already a great
number of proselytes, wear blue, and so forth. Nearly a
thousand of these enthusiasts paraded the streets with
a tri-color banner to give Ramorino an ovation. Although
he was at home he would not appear in spite of the
shouts of " vive les Polonais," for fear of offending the
government. His adjutant came out and said that the
general was unfortunately unable to receive them, and
begged that they would come another day. But next
morning he had gone to another lodging. A few days
later an enormous mob gathered outside the Pantheon,
marched across the Seine towards Ramorino's house,
like an avalanche, increasing in force as they proceeded,
till they reached the Pont neuf where the mounted
gendarmes, after several charges, dispersed them.

---

Warsaw. But he failed shamefully. He might easily have
beaten Rosen and relieved Warsaw; but, owing to his careless-
ness, and neglect of the Commander-in-chief's orders, he did
not reach the besieged city in time. Instead, therefore, of an
ovation he deserved the utmost contempt and reprobation, as
the main cause of the miseries which from that time fell thick
and fast upon Poland. But Nemesis at length overtook him.
In the beginning of 1849, he entered the Sardinian army, and
took the command of the fifth (Lombard) division; but he once
more disobeyed orders, and opened the way for the Austrians
into Piedmont. He was imprisoned, tried by court-martial,
and shot at Piazza d'Armi, near Turin, May 22nd, 1849.

Although many were wounded a fresh crowd assembled on the boulevards under my windows, for the purpose of joining those who came from the other side of the Seine. The police were powerless, the crowd grew larger and larger, until a division of infantry and a squadron of hussars arrived, when the commandant ordered the municipal guard and the troops to clear the streets and arrest the ringleaders. (This is their free nation!)

The panic spread like lightning: the shops were closed, crowds congregated at the corners, and the orderlies were hissed as they galloped about the streets. Every window was crammed with spectators, as on grand fête-days with us, and the uproar lasted from 11 a.m. till 11 p.m. I thought once some mischief might have followed, but about midnight they struck up "allons, enfants de la patrie," and went home. I cannot describe to you the effect of the harsh voices of this excited and discontented mob. Everyone feared the *émeute* would begin again next morning, but it did not. Grenoble alone followed the example of Lyons, but the devil knows what will come of it.

At a theatre, where only dramas have hitherto been performed, the whole history of our late revolution is being given, and people go like mad to see the fights and the national costumes. Mlle. Plater and some other ladies take the names of Lodoiska, Faniska, and Floreska, and a General Gigult appears as brother to Countess Plater.* But nothing amazed me so much

---

* Countess Emilie Plater, a young Polish heroine, who, during the revolution of 1831, served as a soldier, assumed man's attire and entered General Gielgud's division. (The French altered the name to Gigult.) She died during a flight. Her biography has been fully written by Straszewicz.

as the announcement on the play bill of a small theatre that the mazurka " Dabrowski, Poland is not lost yet," would be performed during the entr'actes.

All I can tell you about my concert is that I must postpone it until January 15th, as the operatic director, Mons. Véron, refuses to let me have a vocalist. There is to be a grand concert to-day at the Italian opera house, in which Malibran, Rubini, Lablache, Santini, Madame Raimbaux, Madame Schröder, and Madame Casadory are to appear; Herz and Bériot, with whom Madame Malibran is in love, will assist in the instrumental portion.

Oh, how I wish you were with me . . . . You cannot think how wretched it makes me to have no one to whom I can unbosom myself. You know how fond I am of society, and how easily I make acquaintances. I have scores of such friends now, but no one with whom I can sigh. My heart is, so to speak, always beating in " syncopation," which torments me, and makes me seek for a pause, for solitude, so that no one could see me or speak to me all day. It is most disagreeable that while I am writing to you, the bell rings and some tedious visitor is announced. Just as I was going to describe to you a ball, at which I met a divine creature with a rose in her dark hair, your letter arrived. All the creations of my fancy disappeared; my thoughts fly to you, I take your hand and weep . . . . . When shall we meet again ? . . . Perhaps never, for in all seriousness my health is miserable. I seem merry enough perhaps, especially when among friends, but there is something constantly troubling me within: melancholy forebodings, restlessness, bad dreams, sleeplessness, yearning, no pleasure in life, and indifference to death. It often seems to me as if a torpor came over my spirits; a heavenly calm descends on my head, and images I cannot get rid of haunt my imagination, and harass me beyond measure. In short, it is a mixture of feelings not easily described . . . . Forgive me, dear Titus, for pouring it all out to you, but this is enough . . . . Now I will go and dress for the dinner that our countrymen are giving to-day to Ramorino and Langermann . . . Your letter gave me a great deal of news; you wrote four sides and thirty-seven lines; you have never been so generous before, and I really was so much in need of something when your letter came.

What you say about my artistic career is very true, and I am quite convinced of it myself. I drive in my own carriage, but the coachman is hired. I conclude, or I shall be too late for the post, for I am all in one, master and servant. Take pity on me, and write as often as possible.

Yours till death,

FREDERIC.

# LIST OF CHOPIN'S WORKS.

I. *Works with opus numbers.* *(a) Published in his life-time.*

Op. Nos.

1. Premier Rondeau, C minor.
2. La ci darem la mano, B flat major, varié pour le piano, avec accomp. d'Orchestre.
3. Introduction et Polonaise brillante, C major, pour piano et violincelle.
4. Sonate, C minor, pour le piano (œuvre posthume.)
5. Rondeau à la Mazur, F major, pour le piano.
6. Quatre Mazurkas, F sharp minor, C sharp minor, E major, E flat minor, pour le piano.
7. Cinq Mazurkas, B flat major, A minor, F minor, A flat major, C major.
8. Premier Trio, G minor, pour piano, violin et violincelle.
9. Trois Nocturnes, B minor, E flat major, B major.
10. Douze Grandes Etudes, C major, A minor, E major, C sharp minor, G flat major, E flat minor, C major, F major, F minor, A flat major, E flat major, C minor.
11. Grand Concerto, pour le piano, E minor, avec Orchestre.
12. Variations brillantes, B major, pour le piano, sur le Rondeau favori de Ludovic de Herold. "Je vends des Scapulaires."
13. Grande Fantaisie, A major, pour le piano sur des airs polonais, avec Orchestre.
14. Krakowiak grand rondeau de Concert, F major, pour le piano, avec Orchestre.
15. Trois Nocturnes, F major, F sharp major, G minor, pour le piano.
16. Rondeau, E flat major.
17. Quatre Mazurkas, B major, E minor, A flat major, A minor.
18. Grande Valse brillante, E flat major.
19. Bolero, C major.
20. Premier Scherzo.
21. Second Concerto, F minor, avec Orchestre.
22. Grande Polonaise brillante, E flat major, précédée d'un Andante spianato avec Orchestre.
23. Ballade, G minor.
24. Quatre Mazurkas, G minor, C major, A flat major, B minor.

*Op. Nos.*

25. Douze Etudes, A flat major, F minor, F major, A minor, E minor, G sharp minor, C sharp minor, D flat major, G flat major, B minor, A minor, C minor.
26. Deux Polonaises, C sharp minor, E flat minor.
27. Deux Nocturnes, C sharp minor, D flat major.
28. Vingt quatre Preludes.
29. Impromptu, A flat major.
30. Quatre Mazurkas, C minor, B minor, D flat major, C sharp minor.
31. Deuxième Scherzo, B minor.
32. Deux Nocturnes, B major, A flat major.
33. Quatre Mazurkas, G sharp minor, D major, C major, B minor.
34. Trois Valses brillantes, A flat major, A minor, F major.
35. Sonate, B minor, avec une Marche funèbre.
36. Deuxième Impromptu, F sharp major.
37. Deux Nocturnes, G minor, G major.
38. Deuxième Ballade, F major.
39. Troisième Scherzo, C sharp minor.
40. Deux Polonaises, A major, C minor.
41. Quatre Mazurkas, C sharp minor, E minor, B major, A flat major.
42. Valse, A flat major.
43. Tarantelle, A flat major.
44. Polonaise, F sharp minor.
45. Prelude, C sharp minor.
46. Allegro de Concert, A major.
47. Troisième Ballade, A flat major.
48. Deux Nocturnes, C minor, F sharp minor.
49. Fantaisie, F minor.
50. Trois Mazurkas, G major, A flat major, C sharp minor.
51. Allegro vivace, Troisieme Impromptu, G flat major.
52. Quatrième Ballade, F minor.
53. Huitième Polonaise, A flat major.
54. Scherzo No. 4; E major.
55. Deux Nocturnes, F minor, E flat major.
56. Trois Mazurkas, B major, C major, C minor.
57. Berceuse, D flat major.
58. Sonate, B minor.
59. Trois Mazurkas, A minor, A flat major, F sharp minor.
60. Barcarolle, F sharp major.
61. Polonaise-Fantaisie, A flat major.

Op. Nos.
62. Deux Nocturnes, B major, E major.
63. Trois Mazurkas, B major, F minor, C sharp minor.
64. Trois Valses, D flat major, C sharp minor, A flat major.
65. Sonate, G minor, pour piano et violincelle.

### (b) Posthumous Works.
66. Fantaisie-Impromptu, C sharp minor.
67. Quatre Mazurkas, G major, composed in the year 1835; G minor, 1849; C major, 1835; A minor, 1846.
68. Quatre Mazurkas, C major, 1830; A minor, 1827; F major, 1830; F minor, 1849.
69. Deux Valses, F minor, 1836; B minor, 1829.
70. Trois Valses, G flat major, 1835; F minor, 1843; D flat major, 1830.
71. Trois Polonaises, D minor, 1827; B major, 1828; F minor, 1829.
72. Nocturne, E minor, 1827. Marche funèbre, C minor, 1829, et trois Écossaises, D major, G major, D flat major, 1830.
73. Rondeau, C major, pour deux pianos, 1828.
74. Seventeen Polish Songs (by Witwicki, Mickiewicz, Zaleski, &c.) with pianoforte accompaniment.

### II. Works without Opus Numbers.
Trois nouvelles Etudes, F minor, A flat major, D flat major, extraites de la Méthode des Méthodes.

Grand Duo concertant, E major, pour piano et violincelle sur des thêmes de " Robert le Diable," par F. Chopin et A. Franchomme.

Mazurka, A minor.

Variations, E major, sur un air national allemand.

Hexaméron. The last variation alone No. 6, E major, composed by Chopin.

Mazurka, A minor.

Polonaise G sharp minor.

Valse, E minor.

*Mazurka, F sharp major.

Deux Valses Mélancoliques, F minor, B minor.

* The authorship of this piece is regarded as doubtful.

*⁎* The names of the foreign publishers appended to the above list have been omitted as unnecessary for English readers; nor has it been deemed desirable to give the alphabetical list of persons mentioned in the Work.

G. HILL, STEAM PRINTER, 154, WESTMINSTER BRIDGE ROAD S.E.

# INDEX.